THE LANGUAGE OF FLOWERS 1810-1816

THE LANGUAGE OF FLOWERS 1810-1816

Delachenaye's Abecedaire de Flore and Chambet's Embleme des Fleurs translated from the French

With an introduction and notes by
RACHEL HENRY

Sphinx House

BOOKS BY RACHEL HENRY:

The Language of Flowers and the Victorian Garden

IN THE LANGUAGE OF FLOWERS SERIES

The Language of Flowers 1550-1680
The Language of Flowers 1810-1816

Published by Sphinx House Publishing, Norfolk
Copyright ©Rachel Henry 2023
All rights reserved. No portion of this book may be reproduced in any form or by any means - graphic, electronic or mechanical, including photocopying, recording, taping or information storage and retrieval systems, without the prior permission in writing of the publishers. The author, Rachel Henry, has asserted her right under the Copyright, Designs and Patent Act, 1988, to be identified as the author of this work.

For Eileen Davies
with love and gratitude

Contents

INTRODUCTION	1
ALPHABET OF FLORA, OR LANGUAGE OF FLOWERS	9
FLOWER SYMBOLS; OR THE FLOWER BED	119
INDEX OF PLANT NAMES	183
ACKNOWLEDGMENTS	194

INTRODUCTION

THE EVOLUTION OF THE FLORAL DICTIONARY

The earliest floral dictionaries that I have been able to find were published in France between 1558 and 1671 and were covered in the first volume in this series, *The Language of Flowers 1550-1680*. There then seems to be a long gap until the publication in Paris in 1811 of Delachénaye's *Abécédaire de Flore* and, although he mentions the circulation of lists in recent years, there appears to be no connection between these and the earlier dictionaries. Quite how and why these lists emerged is not explained. It is possible that their authors were inspired by the letters of Lady Mary Wortley Montague, one of which – written in 1716 - described the *selam* apparently used to send messages in Turkish harems. Lady Mary, who learned about this while accompanying her diplomat husband in his travels through the Ottoman Empire sent her correspondent what she described as *"a Turkish love-letter . . . in a little box"*. This consisted not just of flowers but also paper, soap, coal and thread. The significance of the *selam* was discussed in volume one of this series and, while it is unlikely to have been as instrumental in the development of the language of flowers as many people used to think, the very concept of sending messages this way may well have been influential in Western Europe where anything coming from the East was apt to be seen as fascinating and mysterious. In both Japan and China there seems to be a tradition of flower symbolism that goes back centuries. And, according to the novel quoted by Delachénaye in his *Abécédaire* in the section entitled *Observations on emblems, mottos, and the meaning of flowers*, it was also a tradition in India – although whether the specific meanings given by the novel's author are genuine or invented for the story is unclear.

It also seems likely that there were local traditions of floral symbolism in Western Europe (perhaps even relics of the 16th and 17th century floral dictionaries). Delachénaye mentions in the *Observations* section that, in 1720 at the court of Savoy, knights competing in an equestrian event each took the name of a flower with an associated 'motto'.

The lists that were circulating by the early nineteenth century were, according to Delachénaye, at first handwritten and, later, printed, and it is upon these lists that his book is based. However, he is quick to point out that they do not derive from any Oriental list, saying that they have *"neither pretension nor authority, do not come from a real source, and . . . there is great risk that we are deceiving ourselves if we believe what we find in these lists to be the true meaning used in Oriental language"*.

DELACHÉNAYE'S *ABÉCÉDAIRE DE FLORE, OU LANGAGE DES FLEURS*

Delachenaye's book is not entirely devoted to the language of flowers. The first part is concerned with a rather complicated flower alphabet (perhaps better described as a code) which Delachénaye has invented, with each flower representing either a letter or a syllable. These lists have been omitted in the present translation, as they have nothing to do with the language of flowers as we now understand it.

The original book also contains four black and white plates and eight coloured plates. Unfortunately the quality of these precludes their reproduction in the current volume. The black and white plates and seven of the coloured plates have images of flowers, while the final plate shows insects and birds. Each image on the coloured plates has an associated description and the flower descriptions have been included here, although not all these flowers are included in the floral dictionary. The descriptions of birds and insects have been omitted.

This is not a word-for-word translation of the original. Delachénaye seems to take great delight in extremely long, convoluted sentences and the translator has tried to retain the full meaning of his words while, at the same time, making the text readable for a modern audience. Mention needs to be made of the way in which two particular words have been translated. *Floriste* in the eighteenth and nineteenth centuries didn't just mean someone who sold cut flowers but was also applied to the person who grew the flowers and it is in this context that Delachénaye uses the word. It has been translated as 'nurseryman'. Similarly, *amateur* (literally 'lover') does not have the meaning that it does today but relates to those gardeners who, while not nurserymen, had a greater than average interest in plants and were, perhaps, experimenting with different ways of growing them and with developing new varieties. The word has therefore been translated as 'enthusiast'.

Delachénaye declares that he has written his book for women and takes pains in his *Preliminary Discourse* to say that the 'art' that he is proposing can be practised by women of any social class. But his book is clearly addressed to only the upper echelons who have been fortunate enough to receive a good education, as his casual references to artists, authors, Greek mythology and operas reveal.

CHAMBET'S EMBLÊME DES FLEURS

Published five years after Delachénaye's *Abécédaire*, in 1816, this is quite a different type of book. Gone is the emphasis on using flowers (whether in painting or embroidery) in a creative way. The floral dictionary itself is no longer confined to a list at the end of the book but forms the major part of the work, with a description of each flower and a considerable amount poetry. But, like the previous book, there are still many references to Greek mythology and to well-known (and less well-known) writers. The Emperor Napoleon, who was so extolled by Delachénaye, is not mentioned – understandably, since he had been defeated by the British at Waterloo in the previous year and exiled to St. Helena.

Some of the meanings given by Chambet are the same as, or very similar to, those given by Delachénaye. However, it is impossible to tell whether this indicates that Chambet has read Delachénaye's book or whether it means that the lists referred to by Delachénaye were still in circulation and that Chambet has based his dictionary on one or more of these.

ILLUSTRATIONS

Chambet's book is unillustrated but, as mentioned above, Delachénaye's contains twelve plates – four black and white (illustrating his 'alphabet') and eight coloured. In creating this volume, I decided to follow the example set by Delachénaye, with illustrations of some, but not all, the flowers in the book. All the paintings are based on photographs – and acknowledgements for these will be found at the end of the book.

DEDICATION

The title page declares the book to be dedicated to Her Majesty the Empress-Queen. This refers to Empress Marie-Louise, the second wife of Napoleon Bonaparte, the couple having married the previous year. The three page effusive dedication, in which Delachénaye expresses his gratitude to the Empress for being allowed to dedicate the work to her, and in which he describes her as a 'beneficent divinity' has been omitted from the current work.

THE AUTHORS

I have been unable to discover anything about Delachénaye other than his description of himself on the title page of the book: "ex soldier, retired from the Government" which suggests that he went from the army into the civil service and that, having retired, was probably in his 50s or 60s when he wrote this book. He does not seem to have written any other books – or, if he did, they have vanished without trace.

Chambet, on the other hand, was only 24 when his book was published. He lived in Lyon and, as the title page of the book shows, he was a publisher and bookseller (the two professions going hand in hand at this period). He published his first book, a guide to the city of Lyon, in 1815 and was also an essayist and playwright. However, an entry in *Biographie comtemporaine des gens de lettres de Lyon [Contemporary biography of the men of letters of Lyon]* published in 1826 suggests that he was a better bookseller than he was a writer. Chambet died in 1867 at the age of 75.

Abecedaire de Flore
ou
Langage des Fleurs

A NEW METHOD OF REPRESENTING
LETTERS, SYLLABLES AND WORDS
USING FLOWERS.

FOLLOWED BY SOME OBSERVATIONS ON THE
SYMBOLS AND DEVICES, AND THE EMBLEMATIC
SIGNIFICANCE OF A GREAT NUMBER OF
FLOWERS.

DEDICATED TO
H.M. THE EMPRESS-QUEEN

BY B. DELACHENAYE
EX SOLDIER, RETIRED FROM THE GOVERNMENT

PARIS 1811

ALPHABET OF FLORA, OR LANGUAGE OF FLOWERS

PRELIMINARY DISCOURSE

By offering the public an Alphabet of Flowers, the author does not claim to be giving a lesson in botany. To provide new material for almost all the cultured arts, and to present it to the beautiful half of the human race[1] an occupation which unites the useful with the pleasant, is the sole aim that he has set himself.

A new exercise is offered for the reader's imagination, with an alphabet in which the letters and [French] accents are replaced by the prettiest flowers and the most brilliant insects. These, then, can be easily combined to express a beautiful thought, an ingenious motto or a happy verse in a new and pleasing way. It is the author's hope that,

---

1. In other words, to women.

by concentrating on the arrangement of these pretty symbols, a young person will acquire a taste for simple and pure pleasures, while at the same time enriching her mind with the natural history of 96 flowers. The reader will surely agree, therefore, that this exercise deserves as good a reception as most of the skills which we cultivate even though they have no other benefit than vague pleasures and which, far from inspiring emulation, only serve to dull the intelligence and to lead to dissipation.

No invention is entirely new. Each has been derived from a discovery made a long time ago, or from something produced in the past by someone else. The jeweller's newly devised method of forming names with different stones, using the initial letter of the name of each stone, has also been used with flowers – but it should not be thought that this floral alphabet is the same as that. Although the jeweller's system was in use before the *Alphabet of Flora* was published, the author was unaware of it either when he created this method or when he was busy painting the flowers which are the basis of it.

If this were indeed the origin of the *Alphabet of Flora*, one would rightly see it as a simple adoption, and one would learn nothing more from this book than the ability to read the inscription on a ring without the help of the owner – which, in fact, the author doesn't know how to do. But the reader will see that the method introduced here is quite different from such an ephemeral idea, despite the superficial similarity.[2]

Pomp and magnificence appeal mostly to the eye. All the attributes of the most magnificent and brilliant objects can therefore be used advantageously by this new art. It can embellish in many ways. The most

---

2. I suspect that Delachénaye, who is starting to reveal himself as something of a snob, is using 'ephemeral' to suggest 'trivial'.

sought-after flowers, the most brilliant birds, insects and animals – and even man – will be not just ornamental but will form part of a speaking picture.

Neither poetry nor painting can fully express both story and characters. But this alliance of painting and poetry will inspire a thousand new types of activity, from which will arise enjoyment as pure as its source, and within the reach of all classes of people.

But how do we arrange these flowers for this purpose, and yet preserve the grace they derive from nature? Nature herself will answer this question. Ancient walls can be pleasing to the eye but there is neither order nor symmetry in the flowers and plants that grow on them, hiding their dilapidation. Architecture built the walls but a thousand different flowers have planted themselves cheerfully in these cracks, where man would never have thought to have put them. And can we say that they are unharmonious?

If art is only an imitation of nature, it makes sense to look at nature for examples of meaningful pictures. Give a meaning to each flower that decorates the walls of your ancestors' castle and then the flowers in your drawing-room will tell of their deeds, your own exploits, the virtues of a beloved wife, and the annals of all the family.

> *"We have no law like that of the Romans, which ordered patrician families to preserve images of their ancestors. This law of images perpetuated social and political standards; but custom, always more forceful than the law, has preserved, from time immemorial, what we call the family salon. There one contemplated with respect three or four centuries brought together. Families too obscure to be remembered in history at least offered a collection of their*

standards to their children; and the most modest of private standards was no less influential than the example of great deeds. It is to be regretted that our modern salons have been stripped of their ancient finery: for a moment they attract the eyes, but they no longer say anything to the heart. Since we have been affecting, I will not say taste, but passion for the arts, it seems that we want to degrade their use. We would blush to see our great-grandfather wearing his large wig; the shape of his doublet would make us laugh: the young girl would make a joke about her grandmother's wimple rather than think of imitating her conduct. Let us quickly refurbish the family room, and we shall save some standards." [3]

Following this advice would take centuries. In sharing the regrets that the author of these philosophical reflections has expressed about changing fashions, it seems more appropriate, since fashion's empire is indestructible, to make it contribute to compensating the present generation for the loss of family salons. Fashion, in discarding flowers, was blind; it is up to fashion, which is sometimes directed by taste, to recall them.

Flowers are so magnificently adorned just to attract the human eye. The caprice of fashion may well distract our eyes for a moment from the most beautiful ornament on earth; but our eyes find flowers so agreeable and are so powerfully attracted to them that it would be difficult to resist

---

3. Taken from *La Corbeille de Fleurs: Ouvrage de Botanique et de Literature* (1806) by Louis-François-Jauffret & Pierre-Auguste-Marie Miger. [Original footnote]

them.

"*Flowers are such pretty things!*" says Mrs. V. D. C.[4] *"Festivities cannot do without them: they brighten misery and adorn rooms. Like nature, they are above social conventions…"*

If the hand that formed the flowers seems on the whole to have taken pleasure in shaping and colouring them in the manner most likely to delight the eye, why have they been banished from our homes? Let us quickly reinstate flowers on our walls; let them adorn all our furniture. And if they do not make up for all the family pictures, which will perhaps return in the long run with more success than in the past, they will at least contribute, through the *Alphabet of Flora*, to repairing the ravages of fashion and to recalling the taste for moral ideas. By reminding us of the sublime thoughts of our famous writers, flowers will enlarge the narrow limits of our homes; and when winter, or the inclemency of the seasons, brings us back, we will find there these happy vestiges of the beautiful spectacle of nature.

Painting, together with embroidery, will enrich its domain as a result, and we will be able to create large paintings and even entire tapestries. All the decorations will speak to us. An episode by Delille[5] will cover the panelling of a salon. Fragments of Corneille, Racine, Voltaire,[6] will adorn the house of the man of letters. The mirrors of a boudoir, by reflecting a thousand bunches of flowers, will retrace the enchantments

---

4. Victorine de Chastenay in *Calendrier de flore, ou Études de fleurs d'après nature* (1802).

5. Jacques Delille (1738-1813), a French poet.

6. The three great French dramatists of the seventeenth century.

of Armide.[7] The painter, with the help of an eloquent garland, will explain the subject of a painting, and add interest to a portrait's charm, by expressing the sweet thoughts of his model.

Simple flowers, adorned with brilliant insects, in very small frames, will decorate the most modest home, and will propagate in all classes beautiful maxims so appropriate to the maintenance of social order. Although these charming images are less easy to read than the normal alphabet, by catching the eye with their pleasing form, they will perhaps help to bring our attention back to the ideas which they are expressing. In addition, by making us take our time over reading and preventing our tendency to skim through important writings, it may restore to us the habit of contemplation.

[Two short paragraphs, in which the author explains how his choice of illustrations has been affected by the cost of printing, have been omitted here.]

Borders, such as those seen in flowerbeds, are very suitable for creating lines, and the landscapes are very suited to this kind of ornament.

What an interesting scene could be created which represented both the nymphs of the enchanted palace of Armide with all their attractions, and the seductive songs of these appealing sirens![8] The site described by

---

7. An opera by Jean-Baptiste Lully, first performed in 1686 and, in the 18th century, regarded as his masterpiece.

8. The libretto for Lully's opera was based on *Gerusalemme liberate (Jerusalem Delivered)*, a poem by the Italian poet Torquato Tasso (1544-1595), here called La Tasse. The story concerns Renaud, a knight fighting in the Crusades, who is put under a spell by Armide, a sorceress.

Le Tasse in our picture is full of fresh garlands. The flowery woodland, the presence of Renaud's companions whose steps the nymphs want to follow – everything in this subject contributes to the execution of an absolutely new production, which can only be produced thanks to the *Alphabet of Flora*.

There is nothing that cannot be expressed by eloquent flowers, natural or artificial, either with the needle or the brush! And, when we send good wishes at the New Year and on holidays, expressing our thoughts in this way will add so much! Unadorned writings are lost or are put away somewhere, because they lack visual attraction, but the tenderness or friendship expressed by these brilliant illustrations will be something that we shall want to keep looking at.

We see numerous precious objects inscribed with the initial letters of various names, either given as a symbol of love, or just indicating the ownership. But such symbols can't charm us if we view them with indifference.

By substituting flowers, in the way that has been described, we can at least combine the pleasing with the useful. Two flowers grouped together on a snuffbox, on a medallion, or on a seal, will undoubtedly be more pleasing than two letters which are sometimes difficult to distinguish, and whose similarity of form prevents from being rendered clearly.

Young people will appreciate an occupation which allows them to offer tokens of respect and tenderness to their parents – an occupation which is greatly preferable to a wealth of uninteresting and aimless amusements, which simply waste time and leave behind only regrets and, frequently, repentance.

What a difference there is between these false pleasures and all those which the needle and the brush provide! Since they are associated with good habits, one is always sure to see them in the hands of the innocent and the virtuous. Tarquin found the wife of Collatin with his women, busily crafting wool.[9] The wife of William the Conqueror charmed away the cares and troubles of his absence by embroidering the exploits of her illustrious husband.[10] It would be nice to believe that there are still at the court, and in the chateaux, other Lucretias and Matildas.

But is there any need for the *Alphabet of Flora* to paint flowers and embroider them? Without doubt. Vanspaendonck[11], Redouté[12],

---

9. Lucius Tarquinius Collatinus was the son of Lucius Tarquinius Superbus, the legendary seventh king of Rome, said to have died in the 5th century BCE. When Collatinus bragged to friends that his wife Lucretia was more virtuous than theirs, they proceeded to visit all their houses in secret. All the wives except Lucretia were enjoying themselves, but she was busy around the house.

10. William's wife was Matilda of Flanders, and the French sometimes refer to the Bayeux tapestry as *The tapestry of Queen Matilda*. However, modern historians have cast doubt on the idea that she helped to stitch it, or even commissioned it.

11. Gerard van Spaendonck (1746–1822) and his younger brother Cornelis (1756–1839) were Dutch artists, both known for their flower paintings.

12. Pierre-Joseph Redouté (1759–1840), Belgian painter and botanist, is especially known for his watercolours of roses and lilies, and has been called the greatest botanical illustrator of all time.

Vandaël[13], Prévôt [14] and a few others, can, with the most rare talents, express all the feelings of the heart through happy and delicate images.

The needle is capable of emulating the brush, and embroidery with the help of artistically shaded silks has produced the most pleasing pictures. Just think of those masterpieces which compete with the needle of Arachne[15], and the hands of Madame Rousseau[16] and Madame Chomereau, her pupil, whose work with fabrics shows a skill that indicates a keen eye for drawing.

But are the wife, the daughter, or the sister who can only copy always sure of being able to express all the feelings they experience? The sublime is not the prerogative of the many; not every musician can be a composer. On the other hand, with the *Alphabet of Flora,* each of them, who can only draw a flower, can trace without difficulty onto silk, or paint onto vellum, her worries, her fears, her regrets, or her hope.

By painting the dangers facing the hero who makes her happy, the wife associates herself with his glory. On his return the victor will read on a simple canvas the proofs of her most tender love; his children will

---

13. Jan Frans (or Jean-François) van Dael (1764–1840), a Flemish painter of still lifes of flowers and fruit.

14. Jean Louis Prévost, a French still-life painter of flower arrangements whose paintings were so accurate in their detail that they have often been used to illustrate books on botany.

15. In Greek mythology, the highly talented weaver Arachne challenged the goddess Minerva to a competition and was turned into a spider.

16. Employed by Her Majesty the Empress-Queen to teach embroidery. [Original footnote]

carefully preserve these precious fabrics, and will one day show them with pride to their grandchildren, as the glorious testimony of the virtues of their mother.

 How could this pastime not be infinitely recreational? Embroidery has a charm which has always delighted the most illustrious queens and ladies, and the pleasure inspired by the mere presence of flowers is made greater by the satisfaction of giving them expression. Only the favourite of the muses could disdain such delight, and even if it cannot be compared to the exaltation inspired by the fountain of Hypocrene[17] it will never, at least, expose the foolhardy rider to the frequent falls he experiences when he tries to mount Pegasus[18].

Two new roses grown in Brussels last spring have added further richness to this already varied collection! Nature has no need of art, since flowers grow from a simple seed. Such fortunate roses! You owe immortality not so much to the beauty of your forms, to the brightness of your purple or to your picturesque shades, as to the august names bestowed on you by the astonished and charmed gardening enthusiast who grew you. At the first cry of fame, your place was marked in the *Alphabet of Flora*. Before spring returns you to your first splendour and brings you back

---

17. In Greek mythology, Hippocrene was a spring which was sacred to the muses on Mount Helicon.

18. In Greek mythology, Pegasus was a winged horse who created Hippocrene by striking his hoof on the ground.

adorned in your brilliant finery, and long before grafting has multiplied your precious branches, all Europe will have celebrated your happy birth. Alone, you will suffice, without the help of other flowers, to express the cherished names of the Emperor Napoleon and Marie-Louise.[19] [20]

How many times will we associate these great names with these ingenious images, in verses where we will hasten to paint the happiness of these illustrious spouses, in the names of an adored husband, brother, or father!

Thanks to these magnificent roses, a thousand paintings will present the glory of France and the wishes of the world. Rings and medallions will be decorated with the names of the gods who guide us. They will

---

19. Grand Napoléon is recorded as a Gallica Old Rose (a shrub rose) which was grown by the Belgian horticulturalists Messrs. Sevale & Haghen in 1809. It must, therefore, have been developed before the rose dedicated to Empress Marie-Louise as she didn't marry Napoleon until 1810.

20. The Gazette de France of July 3, 1810 announced that MM. Sevales and Haghen, florists *[ie nurserymen]* in Brussels, had just obtained, from seed, two roses which the enthusiasts had named, because of their beauty, the Great Napoleon and Marie-Louise. Without wasting time, the author of *Alphabet of Flora* obtained the drawing of these roses; and after having had them executed life-size, made homage to Her Majesty the Empress and Queen, who condescended to accept them and permit their publication. [Original footnote] *These do not appear as plates in the Abécédaire de Flore and, presumably, were published separately as individual prints.*

adorn the salons, embellish our finery, and will be the joy of family celebrations; and in solemn celebrations, the sight of two roses repeated a thousand times in simple clarity, will excite the most lively joy. Young artists, would you like to paint the hope and happiness of the earth in a single stroke? Bring together the stems of these roses, with a bud springing from their intertwined foliage, and all hearts, without hesitation, will recognise the allegory.

It is from the fruitful source of the good gardener that the author has drawn the description of each flower in the *Alphabet of Flora*. He could not have had recourse to a surer guide with regard to a science that is making new progress every day.[21]

The Latin name given by Linnaeus[22] will be found in each case, next to the common name that the author has often used in the composition of the letters or sounds of the primer [23]. *Le Calendrier de Flore* a work which breathes sentiment, offered him a month's worth of cheerful thoughts which seemed appropriate to his subject, and which he could have adapted, with some success perhaps, to the small number of tables

---

21. Presumably the author is referring here to books on gardening, the implication being that, although he knows how to paint them, he doesn't know a great deal about flowers. It is interesting that mamy of the authors of books on the language of flowers are not, or appear not to be, gardeners – with the notable exception of Henry Phillips whom we will meet later in this series.

22. Carl Linnaeus (1707-1778), Swedish botanist who created the system of classifying plants and animals that is still used today.

23. ie the 'code' or alphabet of flowers in the first part of the book.

which he has indicated in the course of the work.[24] But the fear of seeing such pretty flowers wither on leaving the soil in which they were born must have made him sober in this respect. He was content to glean from a field which presented him with an abundant crop. But he owes no less gratitude to the rich landowner whose beautiful cultivation excited his admiration.

The author was also able to steal from the *Corbeille de Fleurs*, which itself was enriched by borrowings.[25] The care taken to ensure that the beauty and variety of the drawings were perfectly rendered deserves no less praise for M. Bouquet, who directed the engraving, than for Messrs Poiteau and Turpin, who combine to a high degree the science of the botanist with the art of the painter.[26] If the latter had to

---

24. Delachenaye is most likely referring to *Calendrier de Flore (The Calendar of Flora)* by Victorine de Chastenay (whom he has already mentioned) which was published in three volumes in 1802. The book was based on letters Mme. de Chastenay had written to her friend François Beal, describing 400 different flowers. The 'tables' that Delachenaye mentions are probably those setting out his 'alphabet'.

25. The *Corbeille de Fleurs (Basket of Flowers)* by Louis-François Jauffret and Pierre-Auguste-Marie Miger is a book of flower descriptions, poetry and stories that was published in 1807.

26. Pierre-Antoine Poiteau (1766–1854) and Pierre Jean François Turpin (1775-1840), in addition to being botanists were two of the greatest botanical artists of their time. Together they published the now scarce and sought after *Flora Parisiensis*.

combine patience with the most delicate taste to present such small objects in a colouring that recalls nature, the former needed no less experience and skill to overcome the many difficulties he encountered in the arrangement required by such a new work, the success of which depended on precision, and which a single transposition of a flower would have thrown into the greatest disorder.

The same can be said, with the greatest justice, of M. Langlois, whose improvements to colour printing left earlier works far behind.[27] His work required precautions which were all the more elaborate because never, up to the present day, have subjects so small as the flowers, birds, and insects of the *Alphabet of Flora* been printed in colour, and there is no difference between their execution and that of objects of natural size.

The *Alphabet of Flora* would undoubtedly have been better with a more experienced writer. All novelties, the most useful as well as the most trivial, can meet with opposition and it would have been good to support this one with a style analogous to the subject. But not foreseeing that such a light-hearted subject would ever be noticed, since we have arrived here without thinking about it, and having no claim to literary glory, the author hopes that no one will criticise him for trying to increase our enjoyment. His aim will be fulfilled if he has clearly presented the procedures of his method.

Since the *Alphabet of Flora* is less the work of the inventor than that of the authors he consulted and of the distinguished artists who took part in its execution, he also owes tribute (if he is permitted to offer his gratitude) to the kindness of Madame la Comtesse de Luçay (lady in waiting to the

---

27. Langlois was the engraver of the famous roses painted by Pierre Joseph Redouté (1759-1840).

THE LANGUAGE OF FLOWERS 1810–1816

Empress), who, by the rarest benevolence, as much as by love for the arts, has deigned to be his patron!

Love of the arts and of study are linked in this work to taste, morality, and the purest virtue. How could so many standards and merits combined not obtain approval.

NOTE

The next section of the original book consists of 53 pages on Delachénaye's flower alphabet and how to use it, illustrated by four black and white plates. This has all been omitted here as it is, naturally, specific to the French language and, in addition, has no connection with the language of flowers as we understand it nowadays.

The flower illustrations have all been newly created for this edition. Each painting is based on a photograph, for which attributions will be found at the end of the book.

In the following listing, the plants that also appear in the floral dictionary later in the book have an asterisk next to them. The French name of each plant is followed by the botanical name and the English name.

In the original French edition, the order in which the plants are listed has been dictated by the order in which the illustrations appear. In this edition, the order has been changed slightly to accommodate the new illustrations.

In the descriptions, when measurements are given in feet or inches, this refers to the French 'royal' foot and the 'Paris' inch both of which are slightly longer than the foot and inch of the Imperial system used in the UK.

ABÉCÉDAIRE   *Spilanthes acmella*   TOOTHACHE PLANT, BRAZILIAN CRESS[1]

We could not have chosen a plant more appropriate to the title of our work. As its French name indicates, it has spots on its centre, often in the form of letters, . The Latin name *(Spilanthes)* is derived from the Greek, and means flower marked with spots.[2] The plant is a low, creeping annual, and is sown every year at the foot of walls in the south of France. It quickly produces yellow, button-shaped flowers. As the leaves become numerous with crowded florets in the centre, they take on a mottled hue, often forming bizarre figures. This plant is also called Brazil cress, because it has a bitter taste, and is used as a seasoning in Brazil, its native country.

LILAS*   *Syringa*   LILAC

This well-known shrub is native to Persia, from where it was taken to Constantinople. From there, around 1562, it was brought to France

---

1. *Spilanthes oleracea* is also known as *Acmella oleracea.* In India it has been used for centuries to treat dental problems, as it has high concentrations of spilanthol that works as a pain-killer.

2. Actually it means stained flower and comes from the Greek *spiloma*, meaning stain, and *anthos*, meaning flower.

where it has become completely acclimatised. It has also been grown from seed, and by this means several interesting varieties have been obtained. *Syringa media* [3] is known as lilac of Marly because it was planted in abundance in the groves of Marly.[4] Here, in the early spring, it is charming because of the beautiful green of its new foliage and the volume of its thyrses.[5] These are more numerous and have larger flowers of a softer colour than the common lilac, and a scent that is just as sweet, although the tree is of a slightly smaller stature. The famous Swedish botanist Linnaeus, gave the lilac the Latin name *Syringa*, derived from the Greek word *syrinx*, meaning a flute. In Turkey lilac branches have their inner pith removed in order to make flutes.[6]

AMARYLLIS* *Amaryllis formosissima* AMARYLLIS

This name comes from a Greek word *(amarysso)* which means to shine, and is perfectly suited to the *amaryllis-a-fleur-en-croix*[7] otherwise known as the St. James Lily, because its flower, of a velvety red and sprinkled with gold, resembles somewhat the Spanish order of St. James of Calatrava. Its root is a bulb that must be protected from the cold. It is propagated from the bulbs it produces, which, when placed in sandy,

---

3. The species in Delachenaye's illustration.

4. Marly is in northern France, 3km from Valenciennes.

5. Dense clusters of flowers.

6. It is still possible to buy flutes made from lilac wood.

7. Amaryllis with flower in a cross.

smoke-free soil, produce flowers after three years.

BOUTON D'OR* *Ranunculus* BUTTERCUP

The rounded form and brilliant golden yellow colour of the flowers of the creeping buttercup, *Ranunculus repens*, have earned it the light-hearted name of *bouton-d'or*[8]. This wild, single-flowered plant is native to the cool places around Paris. Only the double-flowered variety is grown in gardens. It produces numerous flowers during the month of May but they do not set seeds. The plant can only be propagated by splitting its roots. The *Ranunculus* likes damp places, so it is known in French as *grenouillettes* [9], which is echoed in the Latin word *ranunculus*[10].

COQUELICOT* *Papaver rhœas* POPPY

Every year poppies grow wild in our cornfields where they are noticeable because of the bright colour of their flowers which are red like a cock's comb, from which comes their French name. The poppy is also known as *ponceau*, a word obviously corrupted from the Latin adjective *puniceus*[11] which describes this colour. Sowing poppy seeds in gardens has resulted in stronger plants and, what is even better, an

---

8. Gold button.

9. Frogs.

10. Little frog.

11. Scarlet or crimson.

infinite number of pretty varieties in the flowers – different shades of a single colour, several variegated colours, or one colour bordered with white. Almost all these varieties have double flowers, but they produce seed which must be sown each year in the autumn in order to get stronger plants.

ADONIS D'ÉTÉ *Adonis aestivalis* SUMMER PHEASANT'S-EYE

A pretty annual plant that grows wild in the fields. When brought into our gardens, where it will continue to seed itself, it is noticeable because of the very fine cut of its foliage and the brilliance of its flowers which, although small, are very bright red. The classical poets said that they were tinted with the blood of the beautiful Adonis killed in the hunt by a boar.[12]

CISTE *Cistus* ROCK ROSE

Several shrubs of this name are foreign, and are cultivated for the beauty of their flowers which, by their brilliance and number, make up

---

12. In Greek mythology, Adonis was a mortal who was the lover of the goddess Aphrodite. He was killed by a boar while out hunting.

for the disadvantage that they are so short-lived. *Cistus helianthemum*[13] is a perennial, low, woody plant, which forms fairly large clumps because of the number of its stems and branches. These are covered, throughout the summer, with a large number of white or pinkish flowers which mainly open when it is sunny (reflected in the term *helianthemum* which, in Greek, means sun flower).[14] Native to the southern parts of France, this rock rose has been planted in gardens where it makes a very pretty effect.

DIGITALE POURPRE* *Digitalis purpurea* PURPLE FOXGLOVE

From a rosette of large, green leaves resting on the ground, one or two stems ornamented with a few leaves rise to the height of more than a metre (3 feet) and terminate in a long spike of bell-shaped flowers large enough to receive the tip of a finger like a thimble. Its botanical name comes from the Latin *digitus*, meaning finger. The flowers hang on top of each other, arranged on the same side of the stem, and are a soft purple-pink colour, marked on the inside with darker spots. This beautiful plant, which is found wild in our woods, deserves its place in our gardens where it produces its white-flowered variety. It flowers in the second year and then dies. It is propagated by seeds, which are best sown as soon as they are ripe.

---

13. Also called Helianthemum nummularium.

14. Helios meaning sun, anthos meaning flower.

OEILLET DE LA CHINE* *Dianthus chinensis* China pink

Otherwise known as *Oeillet de la Régence* [15]

The missionaries sent this plant from China at the time of the last Regency [16]. It is a valuable addition to our flowerbeds, adorning them throughout the summer with numerous varieties, all of which are very pretty. Spots of a beautiful velvety red bring out the white or pinkish background of the flower and make them very noticeable. This pink, of which some varieties are double-flowered and yet give seed, is sown in the spring. The young plant needs to be protected from the cold. The following summer it produces flowers in abundance but then dies.

EGLANTIER* *Rosa canina* Dog rose

This species of rose, so common in our hedges, is rightly called dog rose – in other words, good for dogs, because its flowers, although numerous, are small and simple, hardly lasting, and have little

---

15. Regency carnation.

16. 1715 to 1723, when Philippe d'Orléans was Regent during the minority of King Louis XV.

appearance.[17] The plants produce a red fruit, commonly called a rosehip. The whole shrub is covered with very spiky and dangerous thorns. It is not, however, to be disregarded but is valuable in gardens, where it is pruned down to a stem which is allowed to grow to the height necessary for grafting whichever kind of rose one wants.

ÉPHÉMÈRE DE VIRGINIE *Tradescantia ephemerum*[18]
Virginia spiderwort

The word *éphémère*[19] describes everything that lasts only one day, and it is well suited to the flowers of this perennial and lowland plant. The Virginia spiderwort compensates for the short duration of its flowers by the large number it gives at any one time and over a long period. The flowers are of a charming violet blue, which is further enhanced by the golden yellow of the anthers [20]. The plant is propagated by seeds or by splitting its roots. Its leaves are long and narrow like those of grasses.

---

17. Why this should make it a suitable name is unclear. The reason the dog rose got this name is thought to be the belief, in classical times, that the root of the plant could cure someone who had been bitten by a rabid dog.

18. Now *Tradescantia Virginiana.*

19. Ephemeral.

20. The part of the central section of the flower which contains the pollen.

PHLOX *Phlox paniculata* GARDEN PHLOX

The name phlox comes from the Greek *phloga*, meaning flame, and reflects the brightness of the flowers of certain species. All are perennial, and have come to us from the northern parts of America. They are, during the summer season, one of the principal and most pleasing ornaments of our flowerbeds. The flowers of the phlox are numerous, larger than those of the lilac and, like them, arranged in dense clusters. These plants seldom set seed but are propagated by separating the plants in autumn and spring.

FRITILLAIRE IMPÉRIALE *Fritillaria imperialis* CROWN IMPERIAL

This plant deserves its splendid name because of its majestic bearing and its beautiful crown of flowers and handsome tuft of leaves. Although originally from Persia, this lovely plant does not fear our winters, during which its root – a large rounded, white, fleshy mass that smells of garlic – remains hidden in the ground. In the first days of spring, a large, green, succulent stem rises to more than a metre (3 feet). It has leaves at the bottom, is bare in the middle, and is adorned at its tip with 12 to 15 flowers arranged in a circle or crown, as large as tulips and of the same shape. These are of a bright reddish hue which is further enhanced by the tuft of leaves surrounding them. There are double-crowned imperials, varieties with variegated leaves, others with double flowers, and yet others with yellow flowers or of different shades. They are propagated from bulbs.

GRENADIER* *Punica granatum* POMEGRANATE TREE

The Romans first saw this plant in the vicinity of Carthage, and for this reason they gave it the name *Punica*, which means Carthaginian. They called the beautiful red colour of its flowers *puniceus*, and it is from this last word that the French word *ponceau*, which means the same thing, is derived. The pomegranate tree has become acclimatised in the southern regions of France, where it remains in the lowlands. Here, it produces good fruit which is sent to Paris and the north of the country. It should be put in an orangery for the winter, although it will shed its leaves each year no matter where it is put. From early spring it produces new leaves which at first are tinged with red. In July it produces flowers, which everyone knows. Their number and frequency are increased by repeatedly cutting off the small end of the branches and by giving a lot of water to the tree, which needs to be in full sun. The single-flowered pomegranate produces fruit as large as our largest apples, covered with a very firm rind and filled with an infinite number of seeds enveloped in a succulent and slightly acid pulp that is a pleasure to suck. It is because of this quantity of seeds that it has received the *granatum* part of its name,[21] which all the nations of Europe have adapted in their own way. The single-flowered pomegranate can be grown from seeds or from cuttings but the only way to propagate the beautiful double-flowered variety that is so commonly seen in our Paris gardens is through cuttings.

---

21. From the Latin *granum*, meaning seed.

GÉRANIUM À ZONES* *Pelargonium zonale* ZONAL GERANIUM
It is from the Cape of Good Hope that this perennial plant comes to us. It is a little woody and has numerous flowers of a very bright red which shine in our gardens throughout the summer. The seed pods of these flowers grow longer as they mature and then resemble a crane's head, (the Greek word for crane being *geranos*). The leaves of the zonal geranium are somewhat like those of the vine, and are marked with a zone, that is to say a reddish circle. It is unfortunate that with so much merit this geranium has the disadvantage of giving off a very unpleasant smell from all its parts. The plant needs to be put in an orangery in winter, and can be propagated by seeds or cuttings, that is to say by putting the end of a branch in a pot, which is kept in the shade, and which is filled with moistened earth. It will not take long to root and it then needs to be put in the full sun, but care must be taken to water it often.

HÉLIOTROPE DU PÉROU* *Heliotropium arborescens* HELIOTROPE OF PERU
This plant, which does not have a very good appearance, needs to be kept in a pot or container. Its pale blue flowers, which are very small and situated at the end of its branches, would hardly be noticed if they did not give off a sweet scent. The plant can be grown from seeds or cuttings, which take very easily. If care is taken to support the stem and remove the lower branches, the heliotrope can be made into a shrub that can grow to a metre (3 feet) or more. The stem then hardens and becomes wooden. Its head keeps its foliage and can produce flowers during the winter, if the shrub is kept in a temperate heat and left in the open air, making sure that it never freezes. The heliotrope often dies in winter as a result

of cold or damp. In summer it can produce many flowers but only if it is exposed to full sun and given plenty of water. Its name is Greek, and means turning with the sun[22]

VIGNE BLANCHE   *Clematis flammula*   FRAGRANT CLEMATIS

Flammula means little flame [23] and indicates the causticity of this plant which, if put in the mouth, would burn it. As for the word *clematis*, it is Greek and means a small vine shoot [24]. This shrub consists of slender stems, 4 to 5 metres (12 to 15 feet) long, which branch like those of a vine. It also resembles a vine in its numerous twisting tendrils that it uses to hang on, and which makes it suitable for adorning arbours and bowers.

The foliage of *Clematis flammula* is not dense, so it does not provide thick shade, but at least it has the advantage of perfuming the places where it has been planted. It has a multitude of loose clusters and, although the flowers are small, they nevertheless make an effect because of their whiteness and their number. Clematis is grown from seed or

---

22. *Helios* meaning sun, *trope* meaning turn.

23. In Latin.

24. Or simply, a vine.

from cuttings, that is to say by layering its stems and by covering them with soil which are kept wet. At the end of a few months they will have taken root, and will each produce a new plant.

IRIS FLAMBE or IRIS DE GERMANIE* *Iris Germanica*
German iris or Common flag

A mass of fleshy, white, fragrant roots gives rise to short stumps from which arise flattened clumps of long, sword-like leaves. Green stems grow from the middle of these clumps and end in five or six very beautiful, large, very singular, bearded flowers. These may be either a beautiful violet or soft blue, but always with yellow and purple lines and spots. They smell like orange flowers. The plant is perennial and very hardy, and can be found in all gardens. The varied colours of the flowers are similar to those of the rainbow or Iris, which is why they have been given her name [25]. The plant multiplies easily by splitting its roots.

JASMIN D'ESPAGNE* *Jasminum grandiflorum* Spanish jasmine

This is a climbing shrub, native to India, which came to France via Spain. The flowers, larger than those of other jasmine species, are gathered in small bunches. Tinted pink outside, they are pure white inside, which contrasts well with the pretty green of the elegant foliage. Plants are usually sent to us from Genoa, fully grafted onto the ordinary jasmine. During the winter, Spanish jasmine must be kept in the orangery or indoors, and will give off a delicious scent. It can be left

---

25. Iris was the Greek goddess of the rainbow.

outside as long as it does not freeze.

IXIA *Ixia campanulata* CORN LILY

A very large genus from the Cape of Good Hope, of which all the species have a small, plump bulb as their root. The leaves are flat, broad and long. The flowers, which vary in number, size, shade and colour, are all composed of a tube which flares out into six more or less rounded divisions. These are said to have some resemblance to the wheel of the famous Ixion[26]; hence the name Ixia. The cultivation of these plants requires special care, which they repay well. They are grown from seeds and bulbs and must be protected from the slightest frost.

KETMIE *Hibiscus syriacus* HIBISCUS

This shrub was brought from Syria to France at the time of the Crusades. Since then, it has become so naturalised that it does not fear our winters. It is kept in the lowlands where it flourishes during the summer, producing an infinite number and succession of flowers which are large, beautiful, single or double, white or purple, and sometimes variegated with these two colours. It is propagated by seeds

---

26. Ixion was a Thessalian king who, because of his love for the goddess Hera, was bound to a perpetually revolving wheel as punishment by her husband Zeus.

and cuttings.

LIS BLANC* *Lilium candidum* Madonna lily

There is no one who does not know this superb plant which originally came from the Levant and is now well naturalised in our gardens where it is admired for its height and the brilliance of its pure white flowers. From a distance they give off a pleasant orange blossom scent but this can be too strong up close. The root is a scaly bulb which throws out a great number of smaller bulbs to propagate the plant.

LISERON *Convolvulus* Bindweed, Morning glory

The French name reflects the supposed resemblance between the flower of the common bindweed and that of the lily. The Latin name[27] highlights the fact that the plants of this genus twist themselves around whatever is near them. The purple-flowered bindweed, *Convolvulus purpureus*, comes from America, and is now cultivated in many gardens. Its leaves are heart-shaped, and its large, funnel-shaped flowers are very numerous and a pleasant shade of purple.

MARGUERITE* *Bellis perennis* Daisy

This wild flower is commonly found on the banks of ditches and in other damp places. The ancients noticed it and gave it the name of *Bellis*

---

27. From *convolvere* meaning to coil.

to signify its attractiveness.[28] It is also called *pâquerette*[29] in French because, although it grows all year round, it is especially at Easter time that it is covered with flowers. These are small but pretty and of a pure white at first, later tending to turn purple. The daisy has gradually been brought into gardens, where cultivation has not only more than doubled its size but has also varied its colours. In the spring it can be seen in our flowerbeds producing abundant double flowers, some white, others red, others variegated with these two colours, and sometimes with a green heart. All are perennial, and are spread by splitting the roots.

NARCISSUS*   *Narcissus poëticus*   NARCISSE

The poets have claimed that the beautiful Narcissus, seeing himself reflected in the water and dying of love for himself, was changed into this flower. Often indeed the image of this narcissus is reflected in the streams on whose banks it naturally grows. The pure white of its flower, which sways gracefully on a tall, flexible stem, and its pleasant scent have resulted in its being planted in gardens, where it is often seen with a double flower. Its root is a bulb that can be left in the ground. It soon forms large clumps that are even more attractive.

ROSE (à cent feuilles)   *Rosa centifolia*   CABBAGE ROSE

It seems that nature has taken pleasure in creating the queen of the gardens, showering her with its most precious gifts. Elegance in

---

28. From the Latin *bellus* meaning beautiful.

29. From the French *Pâques*, meaning Easter.

her bearing and foliage, grace and beauty in her forms, freshness and sweetness in her colours, delicious scent – the rose has them all. So many beautiful qualities deserve to be sung about; so the poets of all ages have celebrated them. And by ingenious allusion to her charms, to the thorns which defend her, and to her short life, they have made her the emblem of beauty. This flower, which is rightly the beloved flower of ladies, is the first one that one wants to have in one's garden. Fortunately, the shrub produces numerous offshoots from its roots and these can be cut and replanted, making propagation easy.

ORANGER* *Citrus x sinensis* ORANGE TREE

A tree whose graceful and rounded head is at the same time adorned with brilliant leaves of a beautiful green, numerous pure white flowers and a sweet smell, followed by golden fruits whose pleasantly acidic taste perfumes and refreshes the mouth. It is native to India and was brought from various places to Europe, where in the southern parts it is grown outside, while in the northern regions it needs to be brought in during the winter. It is then kept in pots, and special care is given to it, which is rewarded, either by profit for those who possess many of these beautiful trees, or just by the delicious perfume of its flowers, for those who cultivate them only for their own pleasure.

QUINTEFEUILLE *Potentilla* CINQUEFOIL

Although all species of *Potentilla* are known as *quintefeuille*, [30] it is only really appropriate to one – a plant that is very common in our

---

30. Implying that all species have leaves in groups of five.

countryside, and whose leaves are actually composed of five leaflets. The shrubby cinquefoil, *Potentilla fruticosa*, is a pretty shrub of about a metre (3 feet) high. It is native to Siberia and is cultivated because it blooms throughout the summer, with golden flowers in bunches at the end of its numerous branches. Its leaves consist of seven small, whitish-green leaflets. It is propagated by seeds or suckers.

PIVOINE*   *Paeonia officinalis*   PEONY

This beautiful plant has come down from our highest mountains into our gardens, where it dazzles us every year with many superb flowers, which are some of the largest known. They are multi-petalled and a beautiful crimson, or white, or pinkish. The root is perennial and can be split to multiply the plant, which is not difficult but depends on the quality of the soil and the exposure.

RENONCULE DES FLEURISTES*   *Ranunculus asiaticus*
PERSIAN BUTTERCUP

Many species of this genus are used to ornament our gardens but this one deserves preference because of the size and brilliance of its flowers, which may be a very bright red or a beautiful golden or orange yellow. The roots, which in French are called *griffes* [31], are put in the ground in

---

31. Claws.

October. They then need to be covered during the cold season, because they come originally from Asia and Africa. And in the spring they flower. The so-called semi-double varieties are no less sought after. Their flowers charm us, thanks to their infinite variety of shades, or their variegation. Intelligent enthusiasts place them in beds and arrange them in such a way that they complement each other. The semi-doubles can be sown to obtain new varieties. The roots are removed from the ground when the leaves have withered and are often not put back in until the following year . *Ranunculus* is Latin for little frog and reflects the fact that these plants generally like cool soil.

REINE-MARGUERITE*   *Callistephus chinensis*   CHINA ASTER

Not as tall as our great meadow daisy, but more vigorous and bearing more flowers, this plant has earned the title of *Reine* [32] because of the size and brilliance of its single or double flowers. These can be red, white, blue, or various shades and variegations of these colours. The single ones shine with a golden heart. The centre of the double ones is sometimes filled with coloured tubules, known as plush or fluff. It is thanks to the missionaries to China that we have this superb annual plant which, during the autumn and until the frosts come, decorates our flowerbeds which are then so devoid of flowers. Botanists classify the Reine-Marguerite among the asters, and name it, after Linnaeus, *Aster sinensis*[33] or China aster.

---

32. Queen.

33. Nowadays *Callistephus chinensis.*

SCABIEUSE* *Scabiosa* Scabious

If India had not supplied us with the scabious, which is now so common in all our gardens, we should no doubt have had to cultivate the species that grows in profusion in our fields and woods. The common garden variety is known as *fleur de veuve*[34], and botanists call it *Scabiosa atropurpurea*. Both names reflect its very dark purple colour which is, however, brightened by a few pale or white touches. This beautiful plant has the same form as our wild scabious but it is taller, and its flowers spread a light scent of musk or ants. It is sown in the autumn, flowers the following year and then dies. Its name comes from the Latin *scabies*, meaning itch because the roots of one species are reputed to cure this disease[35].

SENSITIVE* *Mimosa pudica* Sensitive plant or Touch-me-not

The sensitive plant indeed seems to be endowed with a sort of modesty, since it withdraws itself from the fingers that touch it. Its branches and leaves then fold back into their joints, only to return to their original position after a certain time. In the warmer parts of America, its native country, it becomes tree-like. In our country, where it can only be kept in a warm greenhouse, it always remains herbaceous. However, it produces pretty clusters of soft grey flax-like flowers, and when the season is favourable it produces good seeds from which it can be propagated.

---

34. Widow's flower.

35. The very itchy skin condition, scabies.

TULIPE DES FLEURISTES* *Tulipa gesneriana* Garden tulip

If we had not imported plants from foreign countries, our gardens would be very poor in fruit and flowers. They would especially lack the versatility of the tulip, which came to us originally from Asia by way of Turkey, where it was given its name because of the supposed resemblance of its calyx[36] to the tulipan or turban, a sort of headdress of the country. It is difficult to describe the beautiful effect of a bed of tulips arranged with taste, with their colours contrasting. It is, however, only through patience, art and care that we have managed to vary the shades of nature's primitive colours. If we had not sown the seeds, we would not have obtained these fresh and well-defined variegations that we admire on the tulip flower. It produces numerous bulbs but these just grow into the same plant. It is necessary to sow seeds in order to have new varieties – but out of a hundred plants, only about two are worth keeping, and even then they have to wait ten years. The bulbs are planted in October and are taken up again in July. They need substantial soil and, above all, soil that has not been smoked for some years.

UVULARIA *Streptopus amplexifolius* Bellflower

The flowers have little appearance, but are arranged in bunches like

---

36. The green part that surrounds the petals when in bud.

grapes and give this plant its name (from *uva*, the Latin for grapes). It grows wild on our high mountains and is cultivated only for curiosity. It will grow in any soil and with any exposure.

VERGE D'OR   *Solidago*   GOLDENROD

One species of *Solidago* quite commonly grows wild in our woods, but it has not been introduced into our gardens because the northern parts of America have offered us plants that are more ornamental. These American species (for example, the goldenrod of Canada, *Solidago Canadensis*) produce large numbers of tall, upright, rod-like stems which, in late summer, have well-filled clusters of small but numerous flowers of a rather brilliant golden yellow. Goldenrod can be grown from seed but, as it is a perennial and forms large clumps, it is easier to divide it. The name *Solidago*[37] comes from the fact that our goldenrod is said to have the power to heal wounds.

YUCCA   *Yucca (genus)*   YUCCA

From the appearance of these plants it is easy to see that they are foreign. In fact they consist first of all of a rounded and symmetrical group of rather firm, long, straight, shaped and pointed leaves like swords. The number of leaves increases as they grow from the middle, while those at the bottom wither. When they fall, they leave their traces on the stem, which rises imperceptibly. When that of the dwarf yucca,

---

37. Latin, meaning *I solidify.*

Yucca gloriosa[38] has reached the height of about a metre (3 feet), a naked stem grows from the middle of its leaves, which sometimes supports more than two hundred white, pink-tinged upside down flowers, shaped like tulips and just as large. This plant comes from South Carolina and, while it is possible to grow it in open ground, it needs good weather. It is safer to keep it in a pot, and to bring it in during the winter. It reproduces by its shoots, which are pulled out and left to dry before being planted. These plants generally do not want much water.

XÉRANTHÈME *Xeranthemum annuum* EVERLASTING

Austria has given us this plant, which holds its own in our gardens, where it needs to be sown every year. It produces varieties with red flowers, others with linen grey flowers, and others with completely white flowers. None are of a very succulent nature (as expressed by their name, coming from the Greek, and meaning dry flower)[39] which means that they can be kept for a long time without wilting. For this reason they are also known in French as *immortelles*. It is these flowers which, when exposed to the vapour of an acid, take on a clear and beautiful shade of crimson – in this state they are used in winter bouquets.

---

38. Spanish dagger.

39. *Xeros* meaning dry and *anthos* meaning flower.

ZINNIA ROUGE *Zinnia peruviana* PERUVIAN ZINNIA

This rather beautiful plant comes from Louisiana. It needs to be sown early every year in a sheltered spot, and then transplanted to a good exposure, when the cold is no longer to be feared. It soon produces an abundance of large radiating flowers of a beautiful blood red, which have the advantage of being long-lasting and keeping their colour until the seeds have matured. There is a variety that has yellow flowers, but these are less striking. This genus was dedicated to the German botanist Zinn, after whom it is named.

MUGUET *Convallaria majalis* LILY OF THE VALLEY

The Latin name implies that it is in the month of May and in the valleys that we should look for the flowers of this pretty plant, which is indeed to be found quite abundantly in the low, cool, and not too open places of our woods. From its trailing roots grow two rather large leaves, enveloping a slender but firm stem, which supports a cluster of six to eight small, bell-shaped flowers of a pure white that is further enhanced by the beautiful green of the leaves. They give out a charming scent, which ladies find very pleasing and the flowers find their way into many bouquets. It can be planted in gardens if there is a suitable place. Enthusiasts mainly like the double-flowered lily of the valley, and the pink-flowered variety.

AIRELLE ANGULEUSE   *Vaccinium myrtillus*   BILBERRY, WHORTLEBERRY

This shrub gets its Latin name because of its resemblance to the myrtle. It was formerly called *Baccinium* because of the great number of berries with which it is loaded[40]. Half a metre or more high (one and a half to two feet), it is very branchy and very full of leaves that are the same shape and size as those of the myrtle. Its numerous white bell-shaped flowers turn into dark blue berries, like those of the myrtle. It is found in the shady parts of woods in Europe. Some enthusiasts cultivate it in their gardens in heathland which is lightly shaded and cool.

FRAISIER*   *Fragaria vesca*   STRAWBERRY

The cool, shady parts of our woods are the natural home of this plant. It makes itself conspicuous by its leaves which are made up of three toothed, wrinkled and beautifully green leaflets, its pretty and abundant white flowers and, above all, its fruits. Usually a beautiful red colour, the fruit is always full of a tasty and fragrant juice. When moved to our vegetable gardens and cultivated with care, the strawberry plant has become more beautiful and more fertile. It is propagated from seeds and often from the runners that it throws out which, taking root in the places where they touch the ground, make new plants which then multiply in the same way. The alpine strawberry, known as the four seasons strawberry, deserves preference because, although its fruit is smaller, it is more fragrant and bears fruit over a longer period. Varieties include one without runners, one that has one leaf, and one with double flowers.

---

40. Latin *bacca* means berry.

BALSAMINE DES JARDINS*   *Impatiens balsamina*   Garden balsam

This is a beautiful herbaceous annual, which needs to be sown early in a container and under cover, and then transplanted into beds with good exposure. It soon grows into a good sized clump, and its beautiful green foliage is enlivened by the bright colours of its flowers which are double or single, red, purple or white, or variegated in a combination of these colours. The plants develop green pods which, when ripe, throw their seeds far and wide, or suddenly curl up when touched. This is where the name *impatiens* comes from. The second part of its name comes from the use that the ancients made of it in certain soothing medical concoctions.

DICTAME BLANC   *Dictamnus albus*   White dittany, Fraxinella, Burning bush

The leaves of this plant are composed of leaflets. Their similarity to those of the ash tree (which in Latin is *fraxinus*) have led to the name Fraxinella being given to this very beautiful plant. It is found throughout the south of Europe and even in France itself. In gardens it needs substantial fresh soil and exposure to the sun. It will then form large clumps, loaded with long stems of very beautiful crimson or white flowers. These give off a pleasant aromatic scent which is strong and subtle enough to catch fire if, in the evening after a hot and sunny day, one approaches with a lighted candle.[41] The plant is grown from seeds, which take more than a year to sprout, unless they are sown as soon as

---

41. The English name 'burning bush' derives from the volatile oils produced by the plant, which can catch fire readily in hot weather.

they are ripe. It can also be propagated by dividing the roots, which are perennial.

ARGENTINE* *Potentilla anserina* Goosegrass, Silverweed

This small perennial plant is found in meadows and on the edges of ditches. Its branches and leaves creep along the ground. The leaves are a rather dark green above, and silvery white below. The flowers, which are quite large and fairly abundant, are bright golden yellow and attractive to the eye.

AUBÉPINE* *Crataegus monogyna* Hawthorn

The French name, equivalent to *white thorn*, and which has been corrupted by the masses into *noble thorn*, belongs to a tree of medium size which grows wild in our forests. It is commonly used to form hedges and is very suitable for this purpose since it has strong thorns and is able to form a bush, producing long, twining branches from the bottom of its stem. Everyone knows that in the spring it is the delight of our countryside with its numerous garlands of pretty and very sweetly scented white flowers. The plant produces bright red berries which adorn the autumn, and provide food for the blackbirds and other birds in the winter. The hawthorn is used in ornamental groves where it is mixed with its double-flowered but unscented variety, and with Mahon's hawthorn or pink-flowered hawthorn, one variety of which has double flowers.

RAMEAU D'OR[42]   Yellow wallflower

This is a very appropriate name for this variety of the yellow wallflower, otherwise known in French as the *violier*, whose flowers are very large and full, and form a long spike of pure golden yellow. Such a beautiful plant deserves to be cared for and propagated. Enthusiasts take care to grow it each year from cuttings. The method for doing this is as follows: in May, choose branches which will not produce flowers and tear them off, with a little heel, from the top of the branches. Cut off the lower leaves, then simply put them in a bowl full of good soil, and water it copiously to ensure it reaches the cuttings. Once this is done, put the bowl in a shady position for fifteen days, then move it into the sun. When the cuttings have taken root, separate them without removing the stems, and plant each one in a pot, protected from frost. With such care, one will be sure to have very beautiful plants in the spring, and these will give many beautiful flowering branches. They last four or five years, and can only be propagated in this way, because they do not produce seeds.

NAPEL   *Aconitum napellus*   Aconite, Monkshood

This is the distinctive name of a species of aconite whose large perennial root is shaped like a small turnip, *napellus*[43]. It grows naturally

---

42. Literally *golden bough*.

43. The Latin word for turnip is *napus*.

in stony places on our mountains. Monkshood, when transferred into our gardens, behaves very well there. During the summer it becomes one of the most beautiful ornaments, thanks to its many tall stems, the upper sections of which are all furnished with a pyramid of numerous flowers. These flowers, which are rather large and shaped like helmets, are of a superb blue. Monkshood can be grown from seed or propagated by dividing its roots.

ECHELLE-DE-JACOB *Polemonium caeruleum* JACOB'S LADDER

This light-hearted name is given to the blue *polemonium* because of the ladder-like arrangement of its leaves. It was brought to France from Greece where it grows wild. It has been cultivated in gardens because, being perennial and very beautiful, it produces spikes of blue flowers over a long period. It is not difficult to grow and is content with any garden soil and any exposure that is not too far north. It can be grown from seed, or its clumps can be split up.

SOLEIL or TOURNESOL* *Helianthus annuus* SUNFLOWER

The flowerhead is the largest known – often more than 32 centimetres (a foot) wide – and consists of a round, brown disc surrounded by ray-like petals of a very bright golden yellow.[44] When its centre is filled with smaller petals it is known as double, and it resembles the sun even more closely. The plant, although native to Peru, grows in our climate

---

44. Nowadays, we know that the sunflower would be beaten hands down by the rare *Rafflesia arnoldii* (appropriately known as Monster flower) whose flowerheads can be over three feet wide.

without much difficulty. Every year it is sown in the spring, and in less than two months it will already have grown a thick stem, more than 2 metres (6 feet) high. In July its stem and branches are topped by flowers, those which are attached to the main stem being the largest. It has been observed that they always face the sun and turn with it.

CHRYSANTHÈME CARÉNÉ *Chrysanthemum carinatum*
TRICOLOUR DAISY

This rather beautiful and rather ornamental flower has white ray-like petals, all marked at the base with a yellow spot, and forming a ring around a brown disc. An annual plant, native to Barbary[45], its stems and trailing branches are adorned with a very fine, very pretty foliage which leaves an unpleasant smell on the hand if touched. In the spring, sowing a few seeds in a good position will result in a pleasing clump full of flowers. Chrysanthemum means golden flower in Greek[46], a name that suits the ordinary chrysanthemum, with its yellow flowers, rather better.

OREILLE-D'OURS *Primula auricula* AURICULA, BEAR'S EAR

This plant, although not very tall, makes itself conspicuous by the bunches of pretty flowers it produces in spring and often again in autumn. It has been brought down from our high mountains into our gardens, where cultivation has perfected it. It rewards the care of the enthusiast who develops new varieties, either in the number and volume

---

45. North Africa.

46. *Chrysos* meaning gold and *anthemon* meaning flower.

of the flowers, or in the richness or arrangement of the colours, which are shaded in a thousand ways and always velvety. These charming flowers grow in bunches at the end of a short stem, which emerges from a rosette of leaves formed in the shape of ears. These leaves sometimes appear powdery or are simply bordered with short hairs. The auricula is the delight of the enthusiast who keeps it in a pot and places it on a shady stage to enjoy it more and for longer. [47]

PERVENCHE (GRANDE)* *Vinca major* GREATER PERIWINKLE

This plant, native to the shady places of our forests, has green, slender, very long stems that spread along the ground, and easily take root. They keep their beautiful shiny leaves at all times and produce quite large, pale blue flowers almost all year round, but especially in spring. There are also varieties with purple or white flowers, either single or double. The periwinkle can be used to advantage to decorate groves and rock gardens.

PRIME-VÈRE* *Primula veris* PRIMROSE

The name given to this plant reminds us that its flowers are the messengers of spring. From the first days of March until the end of April, the numerous varieties collected by gardening enthusiasts display the richness of their beautiful colours. The wild species is found abundantly in our meadows and on our high mountains, but the flowers are of just one colour. Cultivation has perfected them to the point where some people prefer primroses to auriculas, whose cultivation is more difficult.

---

47. Auricula stages or 'theatres' were shelved display units which became very popular in the nineteenth century.

Cultivated primroses offer single and double-flowered varieties in all shades. By sowing seeds, new varieties are obtained, while splitting the roots will propagate the same type. Some varieties produce flowers all year round.

CYCLAMEN D'EUROPE   *Cyclamen purpurascens, C. hederifolium* or *C. repandum*[48]   CYCLAMEN

A low but very extensive clump of heart-shaped leaves, dark green in the centre and bordered with white symmetrical variegation, would be enough recommendation to make this plant welcome in gardens. But to this is added, first in spring, and again in autumn, a great number of pretty, upturned, very remarkable white or pinkish flowers. They last a long time; and when they have withered their stem or tail turns in a spiral, and goes into the earth to carry its seeds, which ripen there and make new plants. It is from this disposition of the flower stalks to roll in concentric circles that the name of cyclamen has been given to this plant.[49]   The

---

48. Delachenaye identifies this plant as *Cyclamen europæum* which is a name that has been applied to all three of these species.

49. The name is derived from the Greek *kyklos,* meaning a circle, but actually this refers to the plant's round tubers and not to the stalks.

plant is also known as *pain-de-pourceau*[50], because this animal greedily seeks out the root, which is large and fleshy. Cyclamen grows naturally in the shady woods of the south of France, and does very well in our gardens if given a shady spot and a light, fresh soil.

OEILLET*   *Dianthus caryophyllus*   CARNATION

Although it has neither the grace of the rose nor the brilliance of the peony, nor yet the majesty of the lily, the peculiar charms of the carnation mean it is cherished, and encourage some enthusiasts to cultivate it exclusively. From the centre of a tuft of narrow, bluish-green and floury leaves, rise gnarled stems that need to be supported. At the end of these, towards the middle of June, flowers grow which are wrapped in a long tubular calyx[51], from which the numerous petals, large or small according to the species, spread out in a circle. They are velvety and infinitely varied in colour and shade, sometimes of a single colour but at other times having two, three or even four distinct colours. A flower that combines so many virtues needs a beautiful name. *Dianthus* means 'flower of Jupiter' or 'worthy of the gods'[52]. *Caryophyllus* is the ancient name of the clove and is appropriate because this is, indeed, what the carnation smells of. Seeds are sown to obtain new varieties, while established varieties can be propagated from cuttings.

---

50. Pig's bread. A colloquial English name for cyclamen is sowbread.

51. The green cup that surrounds the bud.

52. Actually it means 'divine flower' from the Greek word *dios* (divine) and *anthos* (flower).

NÉRIETTE   *Epilobium angustifolium*   Fireweed, Great willowherb

This plant grows wild in cool and even watery places and it has been introduced into the same situations in our large landscaped gardens. It is very effective there, thanks to the number and height of its stems. These are rather similar to willow sprays which earned it the French name of *osier-fleuri*[53]. Throughout the summer each stem ends in a long cluster of burgundy-coloured flowers which bear some resemblance to those of the oleander. This plant has perennial roots, which can grow to the point of being inconvenient.

EUPATOIRE   *Eupatorium cannabinum*   Hemp agrimony

This is another inhabitant of watery places and, as such, it is suitable for decorating and giving variety to the water's edge in large gardens. It will form clumps that are quite high and thick with, towards the end of the summer, numerous stems crowned with purple flowers. These flowers are very small, it is true, but they gather together forming corymbs[54] or types of parasols. The plant is perennial and is propagated by dividing the roots. The ancients dedicated it to Mithridates, king of

---

53. Flowering willow.

54. Flower clusters whose lower stalks are proportionally longer so that the flowers form a flat or slightly convex head.

Pontus, and named it *Eupator*, that is, good father[55].

OEIL-DE-CHRIST   *Aster amellus*   EUROPEAN MICHAELMAS DAISY

This plant has been found growing wild in the Alps of Switzerland and Italy. The abundance and beauty of its flowers have resulted in its being introduced into gardens, where it is easily multiplied by dividing its roots. The plants put out many straight stems which, at the end of the summer, bear flowers similar in shape to the sunflower, but much smaller. Violet-blue ray-like petals surrounding a golden yellow disc makes them look like an eye or a star This is where the French name comes from.

CHÈVRE-FEUILLE   *Lonicera caprifolium*   HONEYSUCKLE

There is in our woods a species of honeysuckle which would have had a place in the gardens had not the species which we represent here been preferable because of its more abundant flowers which have both a brighter colour and a more agreeable smell. Its long, spreading branches make it suitable for covering bowers, and the evergreen variety, on which bunches of flowers are often found in winter, is preferred. This species and its varieties grow naturally in the south of France.

---

55. Mithridates VI (also spelled Mithradates) was king of Pontus in Asia Minor from 120 to 63 BCE. Known as Mithridates VI Eupator, he was a formidable opponent of Rome.

POIS DE SENTEUR* *Lathyrus odoratus* Sweet pea

This plant comes to us from Ceylon[56], and resembles the ordinary pea plant both in form and in size. But it produces abundant flowers, always having two together on a long stem which makes them suitable for putting in bouquets where their bright pink or violet colour, and, especially, their sweet smell makes them very decorative. This pea needs to be sown every year.

TUBÉREUSE* *Polianthes tuberosa* Tuberose

The bulb has a tuberosity which gives the plant its name. When planted in spring, and aided by a little heat, it soon puts out a tuft of long, sword-shaped leaves. From the centre of these rises a stem more than a metre (three feet) high, bearing at its end about twenty lily-like flowers. These are quite large, white, washed with pink at their tips, and having a delicious and penetrating scent. Linnaeus paid tribute to this beautiful plant, which was brought from India, by giving it the Greek name *Polianthes*[57] which means flower worthy of the city.

SYLVIE *Anemone nemorosa* Wood anemone

This is, as its French name and Latin epithet[58] indicate, an inhabitant of our woods. It decorates the cool and shaded parts of gardens, and

---

56. Sri Lanka.

57. From *polis*, city, and *anthos*, flower.

58. The French word *sylve* and the Latin word *nemus* both mean forest.

is enlivened by the beautiful green of its prettily cut foliage and by the brightness of its white flowers. If grown from seed, it can give varieties, either with double flowers, or of different colours. Otherwise the roots can be dug up and planted in suitable situations.[59]

ANCOLIE* *Aquilegia vulgaris* Columbine

Like the many other perennial plants found in our woods, the columbine would have remained there if it had not been for the singularity of its flowers. These consist of five cones or caps, inverted and united, and of a beautiful blue colour. Cultivation has more than doubled its size and varied its colours. White, blue, purple, red and various shades can be seen in gardens. There are also double-flowered ones, which look like small roses because the tips of the caps have been lost. Columbine often self-seeds.

JONQUILLE* *Narcissus jonquilla* Jonquil

There is no spring bouquet that cannot be enhanced and perfumed by the pretty yellow flower of the rush-leaved narcissus, otherwise known as jonquil. It grows from a small, elongated bulb brought to us from the Levant. It is a good idea to take it up at least every two years, separate

---

59. Digging up wild flowers is now illegal in the UK and probably elsewhere.

the cloves and replant them in October in light, unsmoked soil, which is generally the best for bulbs.

IMMORTELLE BLANCHE* or GNAPHALE DE VIRGINIE
Anaphalis margaritacea   COMMON PEARLY EVERLASTING

The French name *immortelle* has been given to several plants which are slightly succulent and whose flowers are able to retain their petals and colours for a long time, even when they are dried out. From the trailing, not very delicate roots of this particular species grow whitish, downy stems (the Greek word *gnaphalion* means a downy plant). These produce white, round, budded flower heads which can be used to make bouquets during the winter.

EPINE-VINETTE*   *Berberis vulgaris*   BARBERRY

This bushy shrub can be found growing wild in rough and uncultivated places that have a temperate climate. The elegance and tender green of its foliage have caused it to be moved into our shrubberies, where it repays well the care it is given. In spring, it is covered with numerous clusters of small flowers whose pretty yellow colour makes a good show. After this, in autumn, it has a large number of bright red, elongated fruits, which are very acid in flavour, but which make delicious jam.

MYRTE   *Myrtus communis*   MYRTLE

A charming shrub which grows wild in Asia and Africa, myrtle was sought after and cultivated by the ancients who made crowns of it for both lovers and drinkers. Its Latin and French names, derived from the Greek word *myron*, which means myrrh or fragrant oil[60], indicate clearly that it spreads around it a sweet scent which the hand picks up from the merest touch. It also has the advantage of being adorned with perpetual and always fresh greenery, on which, throughout the summer, the pretty, fragrant, white flowers with which it is covered stand out. Poets have extolled it over and over again; it is dedicated to the goddess of love. The ladies and the curious in our country still make much of it, but they prefer its double-flowered variety. Both forms are propagated by cuttings, and both need to be placed in a good orangery in winter. In summer they have to be watered frequently and kept in the sun.

ANTHOLYZE ÉCLATANTE   *Watsonia meriana*   WILD WATSONIA

This species, as well as all the others in the genus, comes from the Cape of Good Hope. Its root takes the form of a flattened bulb which, when well cultivated, each year produces rather long leaves in the shape of a sword, and a stem which ends in flowers. The flowers of this species are bright red and are arranged on both sides of the stem. Antholyze is a compound word from

---

60. Actually *myron* means perfume. The word for myrrh is myrrha.

the Greek, and means flower similar to that of the lily[61]. Indeed there are some relations between the two.

POMME D'AMOUR   *Solanum pseudo-capsicum*   JERUSALEM CHERRY

This shrub was brought from Madeira and needs to be kept in a container and brought into an orangery during the winter. Its stem grows to two metres (six feet) in height. Its leaves, which it almost always keeps, are somewhat shaped like those of the willow and are of a dark green colour which contrasts with its numerous small white flowers. These turn into fruits of the shape, size and colour of cherries, which remain on the branches throughout the winter, the season when the shrub is at its best. They contain seeds which are sown to propagate it.

ANEMONE*   *Anemone coronaria*   ANEMONE

Some enthusiasts cultivate this beautiful flower exclusively and with particular care. By growing it from seed they have obtained infinite varieties, both double and single. The two types are very effective in the flower bed when the colours are well contrasted. The roots must be put in the ground in November in order to have flowers in the spring, but as the anemone comes from the Indies and consequently does not like cold or too much humidity, it needs close attention to ensure success.

---

61. Although *anthos* means flower, *lysso* is nothing to do with lilies – it means 'I rage'. The name derives from the fact that the opened flower is said to look like the mouth of an angry animal.

Anemone is a Greek word meaning wind flower[62].

ORNITHOGALE PYRAMIDALE   *Ornithogalum pyramidale*
Pyramidal star-of-Bethlehem

   Although this bulb is native to Portugal, it does not fear our winters. If planted in October, it will grow a stem of about four decimetres (15 inches) in the spring. The end of the stem is loaded with a pyramidal spike of numerous white flowers which form a star and this has earned the plant the trivial names of *épi-de-lait*[63] or *épi-de-la-Vierge*[64]. It is unfortunate that the leaves do not come out with the flowers.

SOUCI D'ESPAGNE[65]   *Calendula officinalis*   Garden marigold or Pot marigold

   This plant is very common, but should not be disregarded since it gives abundant flowers for a long time, even into the winter. The flowers are large, double, and of a beautiful, bright saffron yellow. The plant is hardy and grows well in all kinds of weather, but does best in the sun. It often self-seeds. Its Latin name indicates that its flowers appear in every

---

62. The Greek for wind is *anemos*.

63. Milk ear.

64. Ear of the Virgin.

65. Literally, Spanish marigold.

month[66]. Its French name is corrupted from the Latin *solsequium*[67], because there is one variety that closes whenever the sun does not shine.

PIED D'ALOUETTE*   *Delphinium ajacis*   Larkspur or Delphinium

Our fields provide plenty of food for this wild annual plant, whose finely cut leaves are thought to resemble the long claws of a lark, and whose bud has the rough appearance of a small dolphin (Greek *delphini*, meaning dolphin). The flowers are of a very peculiar shape, ending in a pointed spur. They are of a beautiful blue colour, and have white lines in their background which look like the first three letters of the name of Ajax, AIA. It was this that gave this plant its species name. Cultivation has resulted in many varieties. It can be seen in gardens with double or single flowers, blue, red or white, and in many shades of these colours. A shorter variety has a charming effect in the border.

---

66. From the Latin *kalendae* meaning 'first day of the month.'

67. *Sol* meaning sun and *sequi* meaning follow.

BOULE-DE-NEIGE[68] *   *Viburnum opulus*   Snowball or Guelder rose

The pure white of the flowers and their arrangement in balls or heads, is the reason for the French name of this shrub, which is found growing wild in the damp parts of our forests. It makes our shrubberies delightful in spring. As the flowers of this variety are sterile, it can only be grown from suckers or by taking cuttings.

COQUELOURDE   *Silene coronaria*   Rose campion

This biennial plant is covered with a whitish down, against which the fine crimson colour of its flowers stands out. It grows wild in the countryside, from where it has been brought into gardens. The double-flowered variety is preferred. It is propagated either by taking cuttings or by splitting the roots, but care is needed to prevent it from rotting in the winter dampness.

ULMAIRE   *Filipendula ulmaria*   Meadowsweet

Moist meadows and the banks of rivers and ponds are the places where this perennial plant is found. Its beautiful appearance, its considerable height, and the brilliance of its clusters of very small but numerous white flowers, have resulted in it being given the name of *reine-des-prés*[69]. Its wrinkled and serrated leaves are similar in shape and size to those of the elm (in Latin, *ulmus*), and have led to it being called *ulmaire*. It is grown

---

68. Literally, snowball.

69. Queen of the meadows.

in gardens, but the double-flowered variety is preferred. It can only be propagated by splitting the roots.

PALIURE   *Paliurus spina-christi*   CHRIST'S THORN or JERUSALEM THORN

This is called Christ's thorn because it is believed that the Saviour's crown was made from its branches which have very sharp thorns and are always double, one of them being hooked. This shrub comes from the south of France and stands in the open ground in gardens; it is cultivated there only for curiosity. Its flowers are yellow with very little scent and have little to recommend them. They give a fruit of a rather singular shape which has earned it the French nickname of *porte-chapeau*[70]. It is grown from seed.

QUARANTAIN or GIROFLÉE QUARANTAINE so called because it lasts about this time[71] in all its glory   *Matthiola incana*   TEN WEEKS STOCK or WALLFLOWER

Seeds have to be sown every year, early in the spring, on a warm bed. They soon produce stems full of flowers, either white or bright red, but always with a pleasant clove-like smell. The double-flowered ones are put in the flowerbeds while the single-flowered ones are kept for seed.

---

70. Hat box.

71. Forty days.

RODODENDRON (GRAND) *Rhododendron maximum*
AMERICAN RHODODENDRON or ROSE BAY

This beautiful shrub, with its large, laurel-like leaves, is native to the northern parts of America. In June it is often completely covered by its clusters of pink flowers. It needs acid soil and a cool, shady spot. It is grown either from seeds or by taking cuttings.

RICIN *Ricinus communis* CASTOR OIL PLANT

If this plant, which comes from India, were to be brought into a warm greenhouse, its stem would become woody, and it would last for several years. However, it is treated as an annual because, sown early and in a bed, it produces both flowers and seeds before the bad weather kills it. The seeds look very like the insect which is called a tick (in Latin *ricinus*), which hunting dogs pick up in the woods.[72] The castor-oil tree is only valuable for its unusual appearance. Its thick, reddish stem, covered with a dust similar to that which covers plums, yields a few branches laden with very large, hand-shaped leaves, which has earned it the common name of *palma-Christi*[73]

AMBRETTE or BARBEAU JAUNE *Amberboa moschata*
YELLOW SWEET SULTAN

This is very similar to the cornflower, but larger and of a charming

---

72. The seed has markings and a bump at the end that resemble some types of ticks.

73. Palm of Christ.

shade of lemon, It also has a sweet amber scent. If it is sown in a pot early in the year, protected from frost, and then transplanted at the end of March to a good position, it becomes much more beautiful and produces beautiful flowers in greater abundance. *Amberboi* means 'amber flower' in Turkish. The plant is native to the Levant.

AMARANTE-PASSE-VELOURS or CRETE-DE-COQ *Celosia cristata* Cockscomb

This is an annual plant, native to India, which cannot achieve its full beauty without a great deal of care and warmth. Everyone has seen the beautiful head which, having the appearance of a piece of thick, amaranth-coloured velvet, also forms the shape and folds of an immense cockscomb. This head is composed of thousands of very small flowers, tightly packed together, which keep their brightness for a long time – something that is indicated by the word amaranth which, in Greek, means unfading.[74] It is grown from seed.

HORTENSIA* *Hydrangea macrophylla* Hydrangea

This shrub has recently been introduced from China into the gardens of Europe, where it deserves and holds a distinguished rank partly because of its beautiful foliage, and especially because of the beautiful pinkish colour of its flowers which are arranged much like those of the snowball (*Viburnum opulus*) but in much larger and more numerous heads. It lasts more than two months in its beauty and is often used to decorate homes from which it would have to be excluded if it had the

---

74. Greek *amarantos* meaning unfading and *anthos* meaning flower.

slightest smell. It requires pure acid soil, frequent watering, and shelter from too much sun. It is easily propagated from cuttings. Keeping it in a container and bringing it into the orangery in winter prevents it from having its young shoots destroyed by frost and allows it to bloom more surely, sooner and more abundantly. Its name, derived from the Latin word *hortus*, which means garden[75], reminds us that it makes one of the most beautiful ornaments.

DODÉCATHÉON   *Dodecatheon meadia*   Common shootingstar or Pride of Ohio

The name of this plant is composed of two Greek words meaning twelve deities.[76] But it is too beautiful a name for this small, low plant which produces nothing more than about twelve rose-colored flowers. These are quite pretty, it is true, but small and upside-down. The stem, which is about three decimetres (one foot) high, bare, spindly and straight, starts from the middle of a rosette of rather large leaves lying on the ground. By July, all but the roots have perished. As this plant comes from Virginia, it could well be kept in the open ground, but to enjoy it better, it is kept in a pot. It is propagated by dividing its roots. It was

---

75. "Mrs. Loudon tells us that . . . *H. hortensia*, whose flowers are naturally pale pink, but will change to blue in certain soils, was named after Mme. Hortense Lapeaute, a friend of the naturalist Sir Joseph Banks who brought the plant from China and gave it to the Royal Gardens at Kew." – from *The Language of Flowers and the Victorian Garden.*

76. *Dodeca* meaning 'twelve' and *theos* meaning 'god.'

originally dedicated to the famous English physician Mead, and named *meadia* after him.

DESCRIPTION OF THE ROSES: THE GREAT NAPOLEON AND MARIE LOUISE [77]

The two marvels with which we dare to pay tribute to their Imperial and Royal Majesties, are two roses which are varieties of the *rose de Provins*, known to the botanists as *Rosa Gallica*[78].

The rose *le Grand-Napoléon* is rarely accompanied by buds and seems to indicate by its solitude that the hero to whom it is dedicated has no equal. It is also made worthy of its name by the rarity of its colours and the beauty of its flower, which is double, 50 to 60 millimetres (two to two and a half inches) wide, and whose leaves or petals of the circumference are well fleshed out, of a slate blue glazed with a purplish colour, and surrounding a purple heart which melts into pure violet. It is only after it has been open for a day that the beautiful golden yellow of some stamens can be seen in the centre.

The *Marie-Louise* rose is no less admired for its beautiful shape and the rarity and intensity of its colour. It appears velvety black, although this colour, which is actually a very dark brown, is only on the border of each of the petals, which are all of a pretty purple. This flower is extremely double, 50 millimetres (two inches) wide, and takes the shape of a beautiful buttercup. It is always surrounded by buds, an emblem of

---

77. Napoleon Bonaparte and his second wife married in 1810, the year before this book was published.

78. French rose or apothecary rose.

happy fecundity, and a harbinger of the lasting happiness of the French. The shrub which produces it is less robust, or more delicate than that of the *Grand-Napoleon*. Its leaves are also smaller in size, but they are of a fresh and equally brilliant green.

HYACINTHE* or JACINTHE   *Hyacinthus orientalis*   Hyacinth

This plant displays a thousand varieties of shades of red, blue, purple, violet, white, and even yellow. It often has enormous clusters of flowers of considerable volume which are excessively dense, with heart petals either of a distinct colour or happily married with that of the petals of the head. And, in addition to all that, it has an extremely pleasing scent. These precious qualities have earned a just reputation for this plant, one of the seven which the curious seek so eagerly, and in which they delight. It originally came to us from the Levant. Acclimatised little by little, it is now cultivated with as much care as success by the Dutch who, each year, send us new varieties, with new names, which are always quite sumptuous. The root takes the form of a quite large bulb whose colour varies according to the variety. It should be planted outside in October in order to flower in March or April, although it is better grown in pots kept in the heat of a greenhouse or indoors, as necessary. Bulbs can also be grown in water-filled carafes, which must be renewed from time to time. But those plants that bloom in this way are lost. The poets tell us that this beautiful flower was stained with the blood of the beautiful Hyacinth, whom Apollo killed while throwing the discus.[79]

PIED-DE-GRIFFON *Helleborus foetidus* STINKING HELLEBORE
The French name of this plant comes from the shape of its leaves.[80] These are supported by longish stems and are divided into long, pointed, serrated finger-like sections which are reminiscent of an animal's paw. The scientific name[81] comes from the unpleasant smell of its green flowers. The black-rooted hellebore, *Helleborus niger,* is rightly preferred because its flowers, which are very large and pinkish-white, appear in the middle of winter – which is why they are also known as Christmas roses. These two plants grow wild in the rocky places of our high mountains. They are propagated by splitting the roots.

VIOLETTE* *Viola odorata* VIOLET
Poets and moralists have celebrated this likeable plant with delight, and have made it the emblem of modesty. And indeed what could better

---

79. According to the Greek myth, Hyacinthus was a Spartan prince who was loved by both Apollo, the sun god, and Zephyrus, god of the west wind. Hyacinthus chose Apollo but, when the two were competing with each other at throwing the discus, Zephyrus in a fit of jealousy blew Apollo's discus off course so that it hit Hyacinthus and killed him.

80. Griffin's foot.

81. Literally 'smelly hellebore'.

represent this virtue than the violet, so simple in its ornament, so obscure in its colour – and a flower to which one would pay no attention if it were not for its sweet perfume? It grows wild in our woods, but it could not be left there. Cultivation, by increasing the number and sweet smell of its flowers, has also increased their volume and changed their colours, which can be reddish-purple, pale blue, or white. And all these varieties now have their double-flowered sub-varieties. All are easily propagated by dividing the clumps and separating the roots.

OEILLET-DE-POÈTE* *Dianthus barbatus* SWEET WILLIAM

The flowers of the sweet William are very similar in form to those of the carnation, but smaller, and gathered in a kind of umbel[82] or parasol. Thanks to their form and their beautiful shades of red, they can make a pretty bouquet – hence the French names of *bouquet-tout-fait* and *bouquet-parfait*[83] which are commonly given to this plant. It is found growing wild in rugged, mountainous, and exposed places in several parts of France. Although perennial, or at least triennial, it should be sown every year because that will result in it being more beautiful. It varies a great deal in its shades and in its variegations, which are often velvety. Sometimes its flowers are almost white and sometimes they are double.

---

82. A cluster with a flat or slightly domed top.

83. 'Ready made bouquet' and 'perfect bouquet'.

THE LANGUAGE OF FLOWERS 1810-1816

CHÉLIDOINE *Chelidonium majus* CELANDINE

This plant is very common in uncultivated and shady places, on old walls, and wherever it is allowed to grow. It is well known only because of the stories told about it. It was said that the swallow[84] used it to restore the sight of its blinded young, and this popular tale still gives it the French name of *éclaire*[85]. Its foliage is rather nicely indented, and of a yellowish green. Its flowers are small and yellow and the plant is full of a juice of the same colour. If it is damaged, the juice pours out abundantly and any materials that are soaked in it will be quite strongly stained.

BLUET or BARBEAU* *Centaurea cyanus* CORNFLOWER

This flower is an annual and is very common in our fields. Its beautiful blue colour makes it an ornament liked by both village women and ladies of the city. When brought into our gardens, the cornflower becomes more beautiful and more fertile, because it is not crowded. It has white, purple and various other varieties. Before it opens, the bud appears bearded, because it shows all the hairs that cover the scales of its calyx[86].

---

84. In Greek *chelidoni*.

85. Meaning illuminated.

86. The green part that surrounds the petals when in bud.

It is also known as *casse-lunette*[87] because the ability to cure eye ailments has been attributed to it.

MILLEPERTUIS* *Hypericum* St. John's wort

Mille pertuis means 'a thousand holes', and this name has been given because the leaves of several species are pitted with an infinite number of resinous spots, which appear to be holes and through which one can see daylight. The large-flowered St. John's wort, *Hypericum perforatum*[88] is much sought after for the beauty and appearance of its flowers which are very lovely, very large, and consist of large petals of a very bright yellow. They have a large number of long stamens in the same bright yellow. The plant is native to the Levant, and fears only too much cold. It is propagated by dividing its roots.

At this point Delachenaye includes a short section on insects and birds, in the middle of which he describes one final flower:

PENSÉE* *Viola tricolor* Pansy

This is an annual and low-growing plant which is extremely common in our hedgerows where it has been noticed for the abundance of its small but pretty flowers. It has been sown in gardens, and cultivation has not only considerably increased the size of its flowers, but has also

---

87. Spectacles-breaker.

88. Rose-of-Sharon or Creeping St. John's wort.

varied their shades of soft purple and yellow which is usually bright, and almost always crossed by lines of different colours. The Pyrenees have provided us with a much larger perennial pansy, whose beautiful golden yellow lower petals are enhanced by the soft purple of the upper petals. As it does not produce seeds in our gardens, it can only be propagated by splitting its roots. All pansies have a light and pleasant scent.

OBSERVATIONS ON SYMBOLS, MOTTOS, AND THE MEANING OF FLOWERS

The symbol is a kind of poetry, which uses painting to make its point. It teaches at the same time as it charms the eyes, the image being equivalent to the poet's thought. It is for this reason that Horace[1], wants poetry to imitate painting which, used wisely, makes the observer think and reason.

Before letters were invented, men transmitted their thoughts by means of images such as Egyptian hieroglyphics and the numerous characters still used by the Chinese. Each symbol of their language, which a man could not learn thoroughly in the course of the longest life, represents a feeling or an idea which can be modified by strokes placed variously on the main symbol.[2]

There is reason to believe that symbols and mottos are a modern perfection of these first human notions. It is by means of symbols and mottos that, in recent centuries, morals and politics have been brought to the attention of all civilised peoples, drawing the most useful instructions from nature, history and fable. It was thought that this would gently remove that air of harshness which makes such instructions too severe, and so make easier what is not always easy to understand.

---

1. Quintus Horatius Flaccus (65-8 BCE), a renowned Roman poet.

2. This is a little flight of fancy on Delachénaye's part! While some hieroglyphics and Chinese characters can represent objects, mostly they represent sounds and syllables which are put together to form words.

Thus we have inscriptions which decorate public monuments and offer us moral instructions using the properties of the sun, of shade, of the hours, of fire and of the short duration of flowers, compared with the brevity of life, the rapidity of time, and all our actions.

It may be that painting has more influence than speech on the imagination, or that the soul applies itself more to what comes to it through the eyes than to what it receives through hearing. And it is recognised that a new idea may be more easily grasped if we see it than if we are told about it.

It is undoubtedly for this reason that the heroes of all centuries, after gloriously completing great deeds and famous undertakings, have taken pleasure in instituting festivals and spectacles, in which, by means of a thousand ingenious symbols, people were inspired with gratitude and admiration for their sovereigns.

Louis XIV, in 1662, appeared in a military festival, called a *carrousel*[3] which was given in the Tuileries square, which is still known by this name. There were five square sections[4] but the only symbol worn by the king, who was at the head of the Romans, was that of the sun shining on a globe, with the words *nec pluribus impar*[5] which had been devised for him, and which was a great success. The king's coat of arms, his sculptures, his tapestries and all his furniture were adorned with this motto.

---

3. An equestrian parade or display.

4. Of participants.

5. Like no other.

"Louis XIV was unjustly reproached", says Voltaire[6], "for the pomp of this motto, as if he had chosen it himself".

It would indeed be more appropriate today for the powerful monarch whom victory has crowned a thousand times, and whom fame celebrates in all places[7], than to a young king of France who simply had potential.

These festivals, which were often repeated and sometimes lasted seven days, revived more than ever the taste for mottos and symbols, which the jousting tournaments[8] had once made fashionable, and which had continued after them.

In 1720, according to the Jesuit, Father Menestrier[9], an equestrian event was held at the court of Savoy, where flowers competed for the honour of crowning the Princess of Piedmont on her feast day. Each knight took the name of a flower, with a motto to match.

It is a long time since such things were popular. Even painting, it is said, seems to disdain allegory which, though difficult, is so suitable for exercising the mind, strengthening the judgment, and making ingenuity shine. Like the child who rejects a magnificent toy for a small one that catches his eye, is it in the nature of man to disdain beautiful inventions in order to chase after pleasures that have merit only in novelty? Or does a secret intuition assure him that he can neglect what he possesses, and find a perfection that will satisfy his desires? Let us accept the latter and

---

6. French writer and historian, 1694-1778.

7. A reference to Napoleon.

8. Popular from the 14th to 16th centuries.

9. Claude-François Ménestrier (1631–1705), a French expert on heraldry.

follow the slope to which the taste of the day leads us.

On all sides, we seem to want to borrow the language of flowers from the custom of the Indies, and express our affections with these amiable interpreters.

For some years we have seen catalogues or lists of flowers, accompanied by meanings, which offer the most interesting and delicate allusions to the characters of people and to passions in general.

These lists, at first hand-written, and rare for this reason, have already been made more widely available by printing. But the difference we see in the meaning of some of the flowers leads us to believe that these lists do not come from a real source and have no real authority, and that there is great risk that we are deceiving ourselves if we believe what we find in them is the true meaning used in Oriental language.

There is an episode in *La Chaumière Indienne*[10] written by the romantic author Bernardin de Saint-Pierre, which makes us regret that this distinguished author did not undertake to compose a complete method of such a desired language.

Despite the analogy which one perceives between the meaning of the small number of flowers quoted in the story of the Pariah[11], and that of the flowers which form the lists in question, there is an air of truth in the former. And their application, moreover, is so appropriate that it would be impossible to doubt them if this estimable author had written down the entire collection of the flowers which make up the Oriental language, supposing however that he had ever had the opportunity to enrich European literature with this precious branch of Indian literature.

---

10. *The Indian Cottage*, a novel published in 1790.

11. Outcaste.

So that the reader can judge this conjecture, we reproduce here the interesting story of the wise Pariah of *La Chaumière Indienne*. It will be at least a fragment of the true Indian method, and is very suitable for giving an idea of how flowers can be used to send messages, no matter how authentic their meaning.

"One night when I was at the cemetery of the Brahmins, I saw, in the moonlight, a young Brahmin woman, half covered by her yellow veil. At the sight of a woman of the caste that oppresses me[12], I recoiled in horror. But I approached her with compassion when I saw what she was doing. She put food on a mound which covered the ashes of her mother, who had recently been burned alive, with her dead father's body, according to the custom of her caste. And she burned incense there in her memory. Tears came to my eyes on seeing a person more unfortunate than myself. I said to myself: alas! I am bound by stigma, but you are bound by glory. At least I live peacefully at the bottom of my precipice, while you are still trembling on the edge of yours. The same fate that took your mother away from you also threatens to take you away one day. You have received only one life, and you must die two deaths – if your own death does not bring you to the tomb, the death of your husband will drag you there alive. I was crying, and she was crying. Our eyes, bathed in tears, met and spoke to each other like those of the unfortunate. She turned her eyes away, wrapped herself in her veil and withdrew. The following night, I returned to the same place. This time she had placed a greater supply of food on her mother's tomb – she had judged that I needed it. But, as the Brahmins often poison their funerary dishes to prevent the Pariahs from eating them, to reassure me about hers, she had brought nothing but fruit. I was touched by this sign of humanity and

---

12. The Brahmins are the highest of the castes.

to show her the respect I had for her filial offering, instead of taking her fruit, I added flowers to it. They were poppies, which expressed the part I took in her pain. The following night, I saw with joy that she had approved my token of respect – the poppies had been given water, and she had placed a new basket of fruit at some distance from the tomb. Pity and gratitude emboldened me. As an outcaste I did not dare to speak to her, for fear of compromising her but I undertook, as a man, to express to her all the affections which she aroused in my soul. According to Indian custom, to make my message heard, I used the language of flowers. I added marigolds to the poppies. The next night, I found my poppies and my marigolds bathed in water. The following night I grew bolder. I added to the poppies and marigolds a flower of foulsapatte[13], which is used by shoemakers to dye their leathers black, as the expression of a humble and unhappy love.

The next day, at dawn, I ran to the tomb but I saw that the foulsapatte had withered, because it had not been given water. The following night, I put there, trembling, a tulip, whose red petals and black heart expressed the fires by which I was burned. The next day I found my tulip in the same state as the foulsapatte. I was overwhelmed by grief. However, the next day I brought a rosebud with its thorns, as the symbol of my hopes mingled with many fears. But how great was my despair, when I saw, at

---

13. Hibiscus rosa-sinensis, "The Foulsapatte [is] an Indian word, which signifies the shoemaker's flower from its depositing a black dye when rubbed on leather. This shrub has a fine green foliage, larger than that of the horn-beam, in the midst of which appear flowers, like those of the pink, and of a deep red: they are used in forming close hedges, and there are many varieties of them." (*The History of Mauritius* by Charles Grant 1801).

the first rays of the day, my rosebud far away from the tomb. I thought I would lose my mind. Whatever happened to me, I resolved to speak to her. The following night, as soon as she appeared, I threw myself at her feet, but I remained there speechless while presenting her with my rose. She spoke and said to me: Unfortunate one, you speak to me of love, but soon I will be no more. Following my mother's example, I must accompany my husband, who has just died, to the funeral pyre. I married him when I was a child and he was already old. Farewell. Go away and forget me. In three days I will be only ash. Saying these words she sighed. I was filled with grief and said to her: Unhappy Brahmine, nature has cut the bonds that society has given you. Now break those of superstition by taking me for your husband. What! she replied, weeping, I would escape death only to live with you in disgrace. Ah if you love me, let me die. God forbid, I exclaimed, that I should rescue you from your troubles only to plunge you into mine. Dear Brahmine, let us fly together into the depths of the forests – it is better to trust tigers than men. But heaven, in which I trust, will not abandon us. Let us go. Love, the night, your misfortune, your innocence – everything favours us. Hurry, unfortunate widow! Already your funeral pyre is being prepared, and your dead husband is calling you there. Poor drooping vine, lean on me, I'll be your palm tree. Groaning, she cast a glance at her mother's tomb, then at the sky; and dropping one of her hands into mine, with the other she took my rose. Immediately I seized her by the arm, and we set off on our way."

We have seen in the story of the Pariah that, according to M. Bernardin de Saint-Pierre, single flowers are enough for the language of flowers used in India. The Pariah, wishing to show the young Brahmine the respect he had for her filial offering, instead of taking the fruit which she had placed on her mother's tombstone, added flowers to it. They were poppies, which expressed the part he took in her pain. The following night he undertook to express to the young Brahmine all the affections she aroused in his soul, and added marigolds to the poppies. The next day he joined poppies and marigolds with a flower of hisbiscus, as the expression of a humble and unhappy love. Two days later he placed a tulip on the tomb, whose red petals and black heart expressed the fires by which he was burned. Then he brought a rosebud with its thorns, as the symbol of his hopes mingled with many fears.

We see that only flowers are used in this little correspondence, and that there is not even a mention of the word *selam*, which M. Pixericourt[14], author of *Ruine de Babylone*, a historical melodrama, defines to be: "in Turkey and throughout the Orient, a small bundle consisting of flowers, fruits, wood, and other objects, all of which have an allegorical meaning."

One finds in *The New Eden*, a poem translated from Arabic, a very different definition of *selam*, which is closely related, not only to the language of flowers, according to M. Bernardin de Saint Pierre, but also to symbols taken from the vegetable kingdom, the collection of which can be read below. Here is the exact definition of *selam*: "A *selam* is a bouquet of flowers whose choice and arrangement explains the sentiment to the eyes."

To better realise that the true *selam* is composed only of flowers[15], we simply need to browse the fragments of the Arabic poem, where the

---

14. René-Charles Guilbert de Pixerécourt (1773–1844), a French playwright.

15. This is not something with which Lady Mary Wortley Montague would have agreed – the objects included in her *selam* are discussed in volume 1 of this series, *The Language of Flowers 1550-1680*.

culture of flowers, and the use that was made of them in the most remote times to express sentiments of the heart, are recalled in numerous stanzas. Here are a few taken at random:

I received none of his benevolence,
No present, my sister,
Other than this flattering *selam*;
But this genius will be happy,
That by growing these flowers,
He cultivates our hearts.

Seeing Alzor, my sister,
I was very scared at first!
But seeing him in the rain,
Outside, with no refuge in this city
And trembling for his life
I fly to his aid.

Alzor thanks me
Giving me these flowers
Whose colours he has
Artfully arranged.

He wipes his eyes
And I see tears flowing there.
Your friendship, your extreme zeal
Make me cherish this knot that your hand has made.
By your care, your opinions, my heart is so charmed
That to pick my flowers I only want you.

These flimsy vestiges of a poem written in Arabic, and translated from a manuscript altered by time, cannot, it is true, give a just idea of the composition of the *selam* of the Indies. But they do indicate, at least, that it contained nothing but flowers, and perhaps ribbons, as suggested by the word 'knot' which one reads in the fourth stanza.

Be that as it may, without considering whether the following collection can be used for the composition of a *selam*, by bringing together several flowers to form a message, or whether each flower in the collection can be called a *selam*, we have brought together three different lists, arranging the flowers in these lists in alphabetical order. When the same flower was found in each of the three lists with the same meaning, there was no difficulty. But when the meaning of a flower in one list differed from that in the other two, which agreed with each other, we thought it necessary to adopt this latter meaning. And we obtained by this means quite a long list, since it contains all the flowers in the lists that are circulating, together with their meanings.

NOTE REGARDING MEANINGS IN THE FOLLOWING LIST

Where two or more meanings are given for one plant:

If they are separated by commas – eg Abandonment, neglect – this indicates different translations of a single word or phrase.

If they are separated by full stops   eg To run away. To fear love – this indicates that both meanings appear in the original work.

If an alternative appears in brackets in a phrase – eg First sigh (or breath) of love – this indicates a different translation of that particular word.

SYMBOLS TAKEN FROM THE VEGETABLE KINGDOM

Absinthe
Wormwood *(Artemisia absinthium)*
Absence

Acanthe
Acanthus *(Acanthus mollis)*
Indissoluble knots

Acacia
Acacia *(Acacia)*
Mystery

Aigrette
Thistledown
Desire to please

Aloës
Aloes
Botany

Althéa
Hollyhock *(Alcea rosea)* or mallow *(Malva sylvestris)*
Persuasion

Amandier
Almond tree *(Amygdalus communis)*
Imprudence

Amarante
Amaranth *(Amaranthus)*
Indifference

Amaryllis
Amaryllis *(Amaryllis)*
A coquettish woman

Amomum
Cardamon *(Amomum cardamomum)* – Some early dictionaries translate this as Jamaican pepper, which is allspice
Flattery

Ancolie
Columbine *(Aquilegia vulgaris)*
Hypocrisy

Anémone
Anemone *(Anemone coronaria)*
Abandonment, neglect

Anémone sauvage
Wild anemone *(Anemone nemorosa)*
Illness

Argentine
Silverweed *(Potentilla anserina)*
Timidity

Aubépine
Hawthorn *(Crataegus monogyna)*
Prudence

Baguenaudier
Bladder senna *(Colutea arborescens)*
Laziness

Balsamine
Garden balsam *(Impatiens balsamina)*
Youth

Barbeau-bleu
Cornflower or bluebottle *(Centaurea cyanus)*
Delicacy

Barbeau-bleu des jardins
Cornflower - cultivated
Education

Bâton-des-bergers
Not identified
Priestly power

Basilic
Basil *(Ocimum basilicum)*
Courage

Basil bouquet de
Bouquet of basil
I'm angry

Baume
Balm *(Melissa officinalis)*
Virtue, honesty

Bec-de-grue
Herb robert *(Geranium robertianum)*
Imbecility

Belle-de-jour
Day lily *(Hemerocallis)* or morning glory *(Convolvulus tricolor)*
Coquetry

Belle-de-nuit
Nightshade *(Solanaceae)* or angel trumpets *(Brugmansia)* but also *Mirabilis longiflora* (also called angel trumpets) and *Mirabilis jalapa* (marvel of Peru)
To run away. To fear love

Bouillon-blanc
Great mullein *(Verbascum thapsus)*
Health

Boule-de-neige
Guelder rose *(Viburnum opulus)*
Innocence of childhood

Bourrache
Borage *(Borago officinalis)*
Bluntness, rudeness

Bouton-d'argent
Fair maid of France *(Achillea ptarmica)*
Freedom, candour

Bouton d'or
Buttercup *(Ranunculus)*
Benevolence

Bruyère
Heather *(Erica vulgaris)*
Solitude

Buis
Box *(Buxus sempervirens)*
Solidity. Seniority

Caille-lait
Lady's bedstraw *(Gallium verum)*
Patience

Camomille
Camomile *(Ranunculus)*
Bitterness

Campanelle
Probably bell flower *(Campanula)*
Elegance

Capucine
Nasturtium *(Tropaeolum)*
Banter, jest

Cèdre
Cedar *(Cedrus)*
Majesty

Champignon
Mushroom *(Agaricus bisporus)*
Rapid fortune

Chardon
Thistle *(Carduus* or *Cirsium)*
Criticism

Chélidoine
Celandine *(Chelidonium)*
First sigh (or breath) of love

Chêne
Oak *(Quercus)*
Love of one's country. Power and protection

Chrysanthème
Chrysanthemum *(Chrysanthemum indicum)*
Difficulty

Cheveux-de-vénus
Maidenhair fern *(Adiantum)*
Attire, finery

Chèvre-feuille
Honeysuckle *(Lonicera caprifolium)*
Ties of love

Ciguë
Hemlock *(Conium maculatum)*
Bad behaviour

Cinnamomum
Cinnamon *(Cinnamomum verum)*
Chastity

Citronnelle
Lemon balm *(Melissa officinalis)*
A joke

Citronnier
Lemon tree *(Citrus limon)*
Connection

Clochette
Bell flower *(Campanula)*
A meadow

Cochléaria
Scurvy grass *(Cochlearia officinalis)*
Utility

Convolvulus
Convolvulus *(Convolvulus arvensis)*
Instability. Inconstancy

Coquelicot
Wild poppy *(Papaver rhoeas)*
Rest

Croix-de-Jérusalem
Scarlet lychnis *(Silene chalcedonica)*
Pain, suffering. Travels

THE LANGUAGE OF FLOWERS 1810–1816

Cyprès
Cypress tree *(Cupressus)*
Death. Bereavement

Datura blanc
White thorn apple *(Datura stramonium)*
Science

Datura violet
Purple thorn apple
A clergyman

Dent-de-lion
Dandelion *(Taraxacum)*
You are wasting time

Digitale
Foxglove *(Digitalis purpurea)*
Healthiness

Douce-amère
Bittersweet *(Solanum dulcamara)*
Truth

Ebénier
Ebony tree *(Diospyros)*
Flexibility. Grace

Eglantier
Sweet briar *(Rosa rubiginosa)*
Poetry

Ellébore
Hellebore *(Helleborus)*
Folly

Epine
A thorn
Carelessness

Epine vinette
Barberry *(Berberis vulgaris)*
Remorse

Epis
Ears of corn
Harvest

Faine
Beech mast (or nuts) *(Fagus sylvatica)*
Treason, treachery

Feuille de laurier
Laurel leaf or bay leaf *(Laurus nobilis)*
Certain happiness

Fleur de cerisier
Cherry blossom *(Prunus avium)*
Don't forget me

Fleur de fraisier
Flower of the strawberry plant *(Fragaria × ananassa)*
Perfume

Fleur de lin
Flax flower *(Linum usitatissimum)*
Simplicity

Fleur de morronnier
Chestnut blossom *(Fagus castanea)*
Genius, talent

Fleur d'oranger
Orange blossom *(Citrus × sinensis)*
Generosity. Magnificence

Fleur de passion
Passion flower *(Passiflora)*
The sharp pain of love

Fleur de pêcher
Peach blossom *(Prunus persica)*
Constancy

Frêne
Ash tree *(Fraxinus excelsior)*
Obedience

Fumeterre
Fumitory *(Fumaria officinalis)*
Exercise

Fusain
Spindle tree *(Euonymus europeus)*
Drawing, sketch

Genêt d'Espagne
Broom *(Cytisus scoparius)*
Cleanliness

Genièvre
Juniper *(Juniperus)*
Ingratitude

Géranium
Geranium *(Pelargonium)*
Esteem

Germandrée
Germander *(Teucrium)*
The more I see you the more I love you

Giroflée jaune
Wallflower *(Erysimum cheiri)*
Luxury

Giroflée rouge
Red gillyflower *(Matthiola incana)*
Boredom, weariness

Gramen
Grass
A reward for valour

Grenade fleur
Pomegranate flower *(Punica granatum)*
Perfect friendship

Grenade fruit
Pomegranate fruit
Union

Héliotrope
Heliotrope *(Heliotropium)*
Violent attachment. To love more than yourself

Hépatique
Liverwort *(Marchantiophyta)*
Apathy

Hortensia
Hydrangea *(Hydrangea macrophylla)*
A courageous woman

Houblon
Hops *(Humulus)*
Injustice

Hyacinthe
Hyacinth *(Hyacinthus)*
Love. Chagrin. You love me and give me death

Immortelle
Everlasting *(Gnaphale stoechas*, xeranthemum or amaranth)
Love without end

Impériale
Crown imperial *(Fritillaria imperialis)*
Power

Iris
Iris *(Iris)*
Message

Ivraie
Darnel *(Lolium temulentum)*
Vice, sin

Jasmin blanc
White jasmine *(Jasminum)*
Candour, frankness

Jasmin des açores
Lemon-scented jasmine *(Jasminum azoricum)*
Envy

Jasmin d'espagne
Spanish jasmine *(Jasminum grandiflorum)*
Sensuality

Jasmin de virginie
Trumpet creeper *(Campsis radicans)*
Far away countries

Jasmin jaune
Yellow jasmine
The first langour of love

Jonc
Rush or bulrush *(Juncus)*
Navigation

Jonquille
Jonquil *(Narcissus jonquilla)*
Desires. Pleasures

Joubarbe
House leek *(Sempervivum)*
Spirit

Laurier blanc
White laurel
Candour, frankness

Laurier franc
Laurel *(Laurus nobilis)*
Triumph. Glory

Laurier rose
Oleander *(Nerium oleander)*
Beauty and goodness

Laurier thym
Laurestine *(Viburnum tinus)*
Purity

Lierre
Ivy *(Hedera helix)*
Mutual tenderness (or affection)

Lilas
Lilac *(Syringa)*
First emotion of love

Lis blanc
Madonna lily *(Lilium candidum)*
Candour, frankness. Purity. Greatness

Lis jaune
Yellow lily *(Hemerocallis lilioasphodelus)*
Disquiet, uneasiness

Lis rose
Pink lily
Rarity

Lotus
Lotus *(Nelumbo)*
Eloquence

Marguerite
Daisy *(Bellis perennis)*
Patience. Sadness

Marguerite blanche
Ox eye daisy *(Leucanthemum vulgare)*
I shall think about it

Marguerite reine
China aster *(Callistephus chinensis)*
Autumn

Marjolaine
Marjoram *(Origanum majorana)*
Cheating, fraud

Mauve
Mallow *(Lavatera)*
Humanity

Menthe
Mint *(Mentha)*
Heat, warmth

Mignardise
Garden pink *(Dianthus plumaris)*
Childishness

Mille-pertuis
St John's wort *(Hypericum quadrangulum)*
Originality

Muffle-de-veau
Snapdragon *(Anthirrinum majus)*
Coarseness, rudeness

Myosotis
Forget me not *(Myosotis)*
Remember me

Narcisse
Daffodil   *(Narcissus pseudonarcissus)*
Self-love

Oeillet blanc
White carnation   *(Dianthus caryophyllus)* or pink   *(Dianthus)*
A young girl

Oeillet d'inde
French marigold   *(Tagetes patula)*
A painting

Oeillet de chine
China pink   *(Dianthus chinensis)*
Aversion

Oeillet de poëte
Sweet william   *(Dianthus barbatus)*
Talent

Oeillet panaché
Variegated carnation or pink
Denial of love

Oeillet rose
Pink carnation or pink
Unswerving loyalty

Olive
Olive *(Olea europaea)*
Charity

Olivier
Olive tree
Peace

Orange
Orange *(Citrus × sinensis)*
Sweetness, softness

Oreille-d'ours
Auricula *(Primula auricula)*
Someone seeks to seduce you

Orme
Elm tree *(Ulmus campestris)*
Vigour

Ortie blanche
White dead nettle *(Lamium album)*
Sobriety, temperance

Osier
Willow *(Salix)*
Docility

THE LANGUAGE OF FLOWERS 1810–1816

Palmier
Palm tree *(Arecaceae)*
Dignity

Pavot
Opium poppy *(Papaver somniferum)*
Sleep, sleepiness

Pensée
Pansy *(Viola tricolor)*
I share your feelings

Perce-neige
Snowdrop *(Galanthus nivalis)*
Hope

Persicaire
Water pepper *(Persicaria hydropiper)*
Vigilance

Pervenche
Periwinkle *(Vinca)*
Friendship for life

Peuplier
Poplar tree *(Populus)*
Youthful

Pied-d'alouette
Larkspur *(Delphinium ajacis)*
Lightness

Pin
Pine tree *(Pinus pinea)*
Light, brightness

Pivoine
Peony *(Paeonia lactiflora)*
Heaviness

Platane
Plane tree *(Platanus)*
Shade, umbrage

Pois-de-senteur
Sweet pea *(Lathyrus odoratus)*
Weakness

Primevère
Cowslip *(Primula officinalis)*
Hope. The first flower

Pyramidale
Chimney bellflower *(Campanula pyramidalis)*
Constancy

Reine-des-près
Meadowsweet *(Spiraea ulmaria)*
Authority

Renoncule
Crowfoot or buttercup *(Ranunculus)*
Pride. Impatience

Réséda
Mignonette *(Reseda odorata)*
Momentary happiness

Romarin
Rosemary *(Rosmarinus officinalis)*
Good faith

Ronce
Bramble *(Rubus fructicosus)*
Cares. Jealousy

Rose blanche
White rose
Innocence

Rose blanche desséchée
White rose, dried
Death rather than a loss of innocence

Rose capucine
Austrian copper rose *(Rosa foetida)*
Study, learning

Rose de jardin
Garden rose
Transient beauty

Rose en bouton
Rosebud
A heart that doesn't know love

Rose jaune
Yellow rose
Infidelity

Rose musquée
Musk rose *(Rosa moschata)*
Caprice

Rose panachée
Variegated rose
Summer

Rose sans épine
Thornless rose
A sincere friend

Rose sauvage
Wild rose *(Rosa canina)*
Simplicity

Rose trémière
Hollyhock *(Alcea rosea)*
A housewife

Sauge
Sage *(Salvia officinalis)*
Force, energy, power

Saule pleureur
Weeping willow *(Salix babylonica)*
Bitter grief (or pain)

Sapin
Fir tree *(Abies)*
Fortune

Scabieuse
Scabious *(Scabiosa)*
A sensible (or tender) and unhappy woman

Sceau-de-salomon
Solomon's seal *(Convallaria polygonaetum)*
Secret

Sensitive
Sensitive plant *(Mimosa pudica)*
Secret and profound sensibility

Serpolet
Wild thyme *(Thymus serpyllum)*
A blunder

Soleil
Sunflower *(Helianthus annuus)*
Pride

Sureau
Elder *(Sambucus vulgaris)*
Beneficence

Sycomore
Sycamore tree *(Acer pseudoplatanus)*
Hope and cares

Thlaspie
Pennycress *(Thlaspi arvense)*
Stiffness

Thuya
Thuja *(Thuja occidentalis)*
Old age

Thym
Thyme *(Thymus vulgaris)*
Cooking

Tournesol
Sunflower *(Helianthus annuus)*
My eyes see only you

Troëne
Privet *(Ligustrum vulgare)*
Defence

Tubéreuse
Tuberose *(Polianthes tuberosa)*
Opinion, feeling

Tulipe
Tulip *(Tulipa gesneriana)*
Honesty

Véronique
Speedwell *(Veronica officinalis)*
Sanctity, holiness

Violette double
Double violet *(Viola odorata)*
Mutual friendship

Violette entourée de feuilles
Violet surrounded by leaves
Hidden love

Violette jaune
Yellow violet
Perfect beauty

Violette simple
Single violet
Modesty. Chastity

Embleme des Fleurs, ou Parterre de Flore

THE SYMBOLISM AND THE LANGUAGE OF FLOWERS, THEIR HISTORY AND MYTHOLOGICAL ORIGIN, AS WELL AS THE PRETTIEST VERSES THEY HAVE INSPIRED IN OUR BEST POETS, ETC..

WRITTEN BY

CHARLES JOSEPH CHAMBET
AND EDOUARD M***

LYON

CHAMBET, LIBRAIRE DES THEATRES
RUE LAFOND, NO. 2

1816

FLOWER SYMBOLS; OR THE FLOWER BED

FOREWORD

Among the varied products of the vegetable kingdom, there is none whose sight strikes the senses and the imagination more pleasantly than that of flowers. History and fable have attached great and graceful memories to these light and brilliant beings. It is known that the Greeks and Romans adorned the altars of the gods with them. In holy ceremonies and at meals they made crowns with them. They covered their tables on the days of great solemnities – and they also put flowers on their bridal beds. But, without going back to past centuries, what part do flowers still play today in many parts of the modern world?

The young Indian woman, whose beloved child has died, hangs his body on the branches of an acacia and, while the winds sway his mortal remains over the plains, the attentive mother leans over the bunches of flowers that surround her, seeking to gather into her bosom the soul of her son which a pitiful belief tells her lies on the scarlet petals of the rose, or on the white petals of the superb magnolia.

The language of flowers is known to almost all peoples. Some meanings, associated with tender and painful memories, serve as food for melancholy, but the majority recall ideas of glory and happiness, or make up a mysterious language for the use of lovers, as M. Dupaty[1] has very well said:

> In the bosom of each flower in turn,
> A happy image is placed;
> In a myrtle, we believe we see love,
> We see a memory in the pansy,
> Sweet peace in the olive,
> Hope in the half-closed iris,
> Victory in the laurel,
> A woman in a rose.[2]

In the East the women of the harem have recourse to the ingenious *selam* to talk to their close friends, despite the locks and the watchful guards. (The selam is a bouquet in which each flower has a different meaning, which also varies according to its relative position.)

The little collection we are publishing today is intended especially for ladies. In the flowers which are likely to please them, they find the vivid image of beauty, grace and freshness, and as everyone knows, it is natural to love what resembles us. The writer we have just quoted said, of a sensitive and shy woman:

---

1. Louis Emmanuel Dupaty (1775 – 1851), a French playwright.

2. The meanings for iris and rose given in this verse differ from those given later on by Chambet.

She is a flower just blooming,
Whose pride is a little like the lily,
Whose freshness is like the rose;
Which is like the sunflower in its mobility;
But, unfortunately, a little too lively,
Light as the zephyr,
She takes after the sensitive,
Which withdraws as soon as one wants to pick it.

The author of Clélie, Mlle Scudéry[3], says to beautiful women, regarding flowers:

You may charm, but you will have the fate
Of these flowers so fresh, so beautiful,
Which, however, live for only one morning.
As they please you, you will pass like them.

Finally, the idea of beauty is so closely linked to that of flowers that it is almost impossible to separate them. Hence the famous words of Francis I: *A court without women is like a spring without roses.*

We could have enlarged this volume with a host of exotic flowers, known only to naturalists, and which are more useful in pharmacy than pleasing in their colours and their scent, but we feared (with good reason) to appear too serious in the eyes of the charming class of readers to whom

---

3. Madeleine de Scudéry (1607 – 1701) was a French writer who wrote both under her own name and under the pseudonym of Sapho. She has been described as 'the first bluestocking of France and of the world'.

this work is principally dedicated. We have therefore confined ourselves to short notices on the properties of just a few foreign flowers, as well as on the time when they were brought to Europe. Instead, all our care has been focused on bringing together interesting and little known myths on the origins of flowers, as well as the most graceful verses they have inspired. May this little volume, the fruit of some research, obtain the approval of beauty, and our aim will be fulfilled.

NOTE

In the following listing, an asterisk next to a meaning – for example, Bitterness* - indicates that the meaning given by Chambet is different from that given by Delachénaye. An asterisk next to the name of a plant – for example, **ACONIT*** – indicates that it does not appear in Delachénaye's list.

As with the Delachénaye floral dictionary, where two or more meanings are given for one plant:

If they are separated by commas – eg Abandonment, neglect – this indicates different translations of a single word or phrase.

If they are separated by full stops – eg To run away. To fear love – this indicates that both meanings appear in the original work.

If an alternative appears in brackets in a phrase – eg First sigh (or breath) of love – this indicates a different translation of that particular word.

ABSYNTHE

Wormwood
(Artemisia absinthium)
Bitterness*

This aromatic plant grows in the south of Europe, and contains bitter juices. It is used to make a very well known liqueur.[1] Absynthe looks like a poplar tree in miniature. Its flowers are extremely small.

ACANTHE

Acanthus, Bear's breeches *(Acanthus mollis)*
Indissoluble knots

Virgil tells us that Helen's[2] dress was embroidered with acanthus leaves. Callimachus conceived the idea of the Corinthian capital, after seeing that a basket of jewels, placed as an offering on the tomb of a young

---

1. A green, aniseed-flavoured drink that was very popular with writers and artists (including James Joyce, Edgar Allan Poe, van Gogh and Toulouse-Lautrec) in the late 19th and early 20th centuries. It was banned for a time because it was thought to have dangerous side effects but production began again in the 1990s and it is now freely available.

2. Helen of Troy.

girl, had become surrounded by acanthus leaves.[3]

ACONITE

ACONITE, MONKSHOOD *(Aconitum napellus)*
VENGEANCE

The magicians of Thessaly[4] used this plant in their spells. Its poisonous qualities, according to the ancients, were due to the foam which the dreadful Cerberus spat on it, when Hercules, having triumphed over death and the gods of the underworld, snatched this guardian from the gates of Hades and displayed him, in bonds, to mortal eyes.[5]

AMANDIER

ALMOND TREE *(Prunus dulcis)*
PRUDENCE*[6]

This plant is the first to flower after the frosts and is the symbol of diligence or activity.

---

3. Callimachus was a Greek sculptor who lived in the 5th century BCE and who is credited with designing the Corinthian style of architecture.

4. A region of ancient Greece.

5. Cerberus was the many-headed dog that, in Greek legend, guarded the gates of the Underworld.

6. This reverses Delachénaye's meaning of imprudence.

AMARANTHE

Amaranth

Indifference. Disdain*

Among the ancients, amaranth was a symbol of immortality, no doubt because it retains its colour and does not fade. The melancholy tint of its flowers meant it was chosen in antiquity as a sign of mourning, and people wore crowns of it at funeral feasts. The order of the Knights of the Amarante was instituted by Queen Christina of Sweden in 1653.

AMARYLLIS

Amaryllis

Coquetry [7]

Amaryllis comes from the Greek word *amarysso*, which means to shine,[8] because the flowers of this plant are beautiful. The amaryllis was brought to us from Mexico in 1693. This plant is known under different names in various parts of the world. The variety that grows in France is

---

7. Delachénaye gives it the meaning of a coquettish woman.

8. The Greek word amarysso means "to sparkle," but a Greek myth says the flower sprang up from the blood of a girl of that name who pierced her heart with a golden arrow in order to win the love of a shepherd called Alteo.

known as *amaryllis à fleurs roses*[9] and has flowers that are light purple mixed with white.

ANÉMONE
Anemone
Candour*

In Greek mythology, the anemone was said to have sprung from the blood of Adonis.

The earth, with sorrow, drinks the united streams
Of Venus' tears and Adonis' blood;
With a rose the earth is suddenly crowned
And near her rises a pale anemone. CHAUSSARD[10]

The name of this flower comes from the Greek *anemos* (wind) because it thrives in places exposed to the wind.

Emblem of life, lovely and tender flower,
Which shines in the morning, in the evening loses its colour;

---

9. Amaryllis with pink flowers.

10. Pierre-Jean-Baptiste Chaussard (1766–1823), known as Publicola Chaussard, was a French writer, art critic and poet.

And passing from our meadows to the infernal shore,
Presents to us in a day the fleeting image
Of youth and happiness. DEMOUSTIER[11]

There are a thousand species of anemone. The liverworts[12] alone are worthy of attention. The wood anemone *(sylvae)* gives a large number of pretty white flowers. The wild anemone has the meaning of 'suffering caused by love'.

ANGÉLIQUE*

ANGELICA *(Angelica archangelica)*

ECSTASY

Following the example of the beautiful princess of Cathay whose name it bears, and who preferred, with her lover Medoro. the peace of the forests to the palace of the kings, this plant likes rural places.[13] Wild angelica raises an elegant head on top of a thick, fresh-coloured stem. Within our gardens, it forms massive bushes. There its scent becomes more penetrating, while that of the meadows has little perfume.

A POEM HAS BEEN OMITTED HERE

---

11. Charles-Albert Demoustier (1760 –1801), a French writer.

12. Anemone hepatica.

13. Angelica was the heroine of the poem *Roland Furieux* by Ludovico Ariosto (1474-1533).

ARGENTINE

Silverweed *(Potentilla anserina)*
Pride*

This flower, apart from the colour, is similar to that of the strawberry, and resembles the cinquefoil[14], which has been nicknamed in French 'the yellow strawberry'. The silverweed flower bears a double calyx, one of which droops on the stem, while the other spreads out and descends like a star.

AUBÉPINE

Hawthorn *(Crataegus monogyna)*
Prudence and sincerity*

At weddings in ancient Greece, flowering branches of hawthorn were worn, and the candlesticks which lit the newlyweds on their entry into the nuptial chamber were made of hawthorn wood. This shrub is found in forests. Its white flowers have a very pleasant scent. Two different varieties of hawthorn are also cultivated in our gardens: one, less fragrant but with double flowers, and the other, with single flowers, that are red as soon as they open.

BALSAMINE

Balsam *(Impatiens balsamina)*
Foresight*

Balsam is one of the flowers that is resistant to the heat of summer. It grows to little more than a foot high and has only a few branches. It

---

14. *Potentilla erecta.*

has flowers of eye-catching shades – corollas of a dark crimson striped or speckled with white are common, and we also see shades of violet and a few other tints. It commonly produces a double flower and grows well in our flowerbeds. In fact, nothing seems better arranged, nor more compact, than a fresh balsam.

BASILIC

Basil *(Ocimum basilicum)*
Poverty*

This little plant grows in a tuft and, with a little care, will survive the winter in our climate. Its smell seems to come from its leaf much more than from its flower.

BELLE-DE-NUIT

Angel trumpets
(Mirabilis longiflora)
or Marvel of Peru
(Mirabilis jalapa)
To flee and fear love

Solitary lover of the night,
Why these timid alarms,
When, my muse, the day you flee
Is about to reveal your charms?
If, out of modesty, from prying eyes
You hide your purple flower,
By stealing your attractions,

At least let them be surmised.

When dawn comes to wake

The brilliant daughters of Flora,

Alone, you seem to sleep

And fear the brilliance of the dawn.

When the shadow erases their colours,

You then resume your finery;

And for the absence of your sisters,

You come to console Nature.   CONSTANT DUBOS[15]

This flower avoids the bright light and heat of the day. It closes at nine o'clock in the morning, reopens after sunset, and enjoys the cool of the night.

BELLE-DE-JOUR

MORNING GLORY (*Convolvulus tricolor* or *Ipomoea purpurea*)
INFIDELITY*

Quite unlike the little coquette of which we have just spoken, the *belle-de-jour* opens out in the morning and closes at nightfall. The edges of its flower are blue, the middle white and the centre a sulphur yellow.[16]

If you see some flowers of foreign origin,

Avoiding the glare of light,

---

15. Constant Dubos (1768 - 1845), poet and professor of rhetoric.

16. Although Chambet has now gone on to write about the *belle-de-jour*, the following verse is about the *belle-de-nuit*.

Like the beauties who reign at Court,
Awake by night, sleep by day,
In the places where Europe delighted their childhood,
The day is born, when the night begins. CASTEL[17]

The ingenious idea contained in these verses may serve to explain the habits of the Belle-de-nuit. We find in the West Indies a shrub called *galant de jour*[18] and another, *galant de nuit*,[19] which present the same singularities as the two flowers of which we have just spoken.

M.Philippon-de-la-Madelaine[20] celebrated these two flowers in the following couplets:

The soft rays of dawn
And morning guide my steps.
I see two daughters of Flora,
One hurrying to bloom,
The other veiling her charms.
To the fires whose air sparkles,
The *Belle-de-jour* opens;

---

17. Probably French poet and naturalist René Richard Louis Castel (1758–1832) after whom a genus of shrubs, *Castela*, was named.

18. *Cestrum diurnum* – day jessamine or wild jasmine.

19. *Brunfelsia americana* – trumpet flower – or *Cestrum nocturnum* – night jasmine.

20. Louis Philipon de La Madelaine (1734 –1818), a French writer.

FIVE LINES HAVE BEEN OMITTED HERE

To shine is your supreme art;
Without sparkle, pleasure itself
Becomes unattractive to you.
The other flower, no less pretty,
Flees the brightness of the Heavens.
Your dear companion of the nights,
Seems to us to be hiding her life,
The real secret to being happy.

FIVE LINES HAVE BEEN OMITTED HERE

If there is a desirable fate,
It is to be able to ignite a tender, gentle, affable nymph
Who, by day, knows how to be kind,
And who at night knows how to love.

BOULE-DE-NEIGE

Snowball, Guelder rose *(Viburnum opulus)*

Slander*

We confine ourselves here to giving the following allegory concerning this flower: The snowball, an innocent flower, grew at the foot of a steep mountain. One day she saw, coming off the top of the mountain, a small mass of snow which became larger as it descended. "Well," said the flower, "here is a snowball. As my relative, she will do me no harm." What a fatal mistake! The snowball, becoming larger as it rolled, acquired so much volume, strength, and weight, that, knocking down all the shrubs, it crushed the poor flower. Thus slander, growing from mouth to mouth, does not spare even its relatives.

BOUTON-D'OR[21]

BUTTERCUP
(Ranunculus – several species)
SATISFIED & CONSTANT LOVE*

This pretty satin button,
Who smiles innocently,
Conceals a poisonous juice,
And often hurts recklessness.
CONSTANT DUBOS.

The buttercup is a variety of *Ranunculus*. It flowers in May. This little flower grows wild in the fields, but in our gardens we have different varieties with double flowers.

BLUET or BARBEAU

CORNFLOWER *(Centaurea cyanus)*
DELICACY. MELANCHOLY*

This modest flower, often despised in favour of brighter ones, is nevertheless a pretty symbol of simplicity and innocence.

---

21. Literally 'gold button'.

CAPUCINE

Nasturtium *(Tropaeolum genus)*
Discretion*

The nasturtium, originally from Peru, reminds us of the virgins of the sun[22] and it is always towards the sun that it turns. Several naturalists have observed in this flower a phenomenon which seems to us to be associated with electricity – after sunset, and in the morning before sunrise, the nasturtium flashes like lightning. Like all plants that need support, the nasturtium has round stems, the ends of which roll up and will form knots around whatever they encounter.

CHÈVRE-FEUILLE

Honeysuckle *(Lonicera caprifolium)*
Bonds of love

The honeysuckle offers many variations in its colours. It is a very fragrant flower, which represents simplicity to us, and is used to adorn our thickets and our arbours.

CITRONNIER

Lemon tree
Desire for a connection[23]

In ancient times, people used the fruit of the lemon tree to protect themselves from enchantments. The women bit into it from time to

---

22. Presumably this refers to priestesses of the Inca sun god, Inti.

23. Delachénaye simply gives 'connection' as the meaning.

time to perfume their breath, and to make their lips vermilion. In the Indian provinces when wives burn themselves after the death of their husbands, they throw themselves onto the pyre holding a lemon.

CLOCHETTE

Bell flower *(Campanula and others)*
Chit-chat*

The stem of the bellflower, which is not very tall, is as thin as a thread and bears small leaves. Its flower is a bluish bell of fine texture and a fresh and brilliant shade. We know several varieties of this flower, all as simple as they are pretty.

A SHORT VERSE HAS BEEN OMITTED HERE

COQUELIQUOT

Wild poppy *(Papaver rhoeas)*
Recognition, gratitude*

This flower is found in large numbers in our fields and among the ears of wheat. The young shepherdesses make crowns of it, or adorn their straw hats with it. But this flower is so fragile that the slightest wind is enough to detach the petals from its stem.

COUCOU*

Oxlip *(Primula elatior)*, Primrose *(Primula veris)*
Kidney vetch *(Anthyllis vulneria)*
Bluebell *(Hyacinthoides non scripta)* and White clover [24]
Portent

This spring flower, pleasant and fresh, is found in woods and in meadows. The two shades which colour it are very soft and together they are soothing to the eye. Its flowers are always grouped at the top of a strong and common stem. It flowers in the most deserted places, and braves both frost and bad weather.

COURONNE IMPÉRIALE*

Crown imperial *(Fritillaria imperialis)*
Pride without gentleness

Juno was jealous of the fact that Jupiter had given birth to Minerva, who sprang straight from his brain, and she wanted to become a mother in a less unusual way. She consulted Flora, and this goddess told her that in the fields of Olene there was a flower whose simple touch had the virtue of making someone fertile.[25] Juno touched the flower, and gave birth to the god of war. The ancients believed that the flower that Juno touched was the crown imperial.

---

24. While all of these plants are known as 'coucou', the description given suggests that Chambet is referring to the oxlip.

25. In Greek mythology, Olene was the daughter of the river god Asopus.

Juno, annoyed by Minerva's birth,
In the fields of Olène, one day, in a gloomy silence,
Was wandering, when a flower offered itself to her gaze:
She approaches, bows; towards its stem
She stretches out her hand, O miracle!
The goddess instantly sees the god Mars is born.

This flower, originally from Persia, was brought from Constantinople in the 15th century to the court of Emperor Maximilian II. It only appeared in France in 1570.[26] The scent of this flower is very strong. The plant is believed to be poisonous, and its root, taken internally, produces the same effect as hemlock.

LE GENÉT

Broom *(Cytisus scoparius)*
Feeble hope*

There are more than thirty species of broom growing in Europe. The one which is most commonly employed for the embellishment of groves is the Spanish broom, whose yellow

---

26. Chambet seems to be a little confused here. Maximilian II was Holy Roman Emperor in the 16th century – from 1564 to 1576 – and the first crown imperial plants to be grown outside the Middle East were in Leiden, in the gardens of the botanist Charles de l'Écluse, otherwise known as Carolus Clusius, who lived from 1526 to 1609.

flowers have a sweet scent. They first appear in early summer, and bloom until the end of the season.

GÉRANIUM

Geranium *(Pelargonium)*
Esteem

The geranium is native to the Cape. There are several varieties. The musky geranium's meaning is *esteem*; the pink geranium, *languor*; the lemon geranium, *caprice*; etc.

GERMANDRÉE

Germander *(Teucrium chamaedrys)*
The more I see you the more I love you

Germander is also called *petit chêne*[27], no doubt because of the shape of its leaves which have some resemblance to that of the king of the forests. Its stem is square and reddish, and its flowers are a soft pink.

GIROFLÉE

Wallflower *(Erysimum cheiri)*
or Gillyflower *(Matthiola incana)*
Pleasure*. Sympathy*

---

27. Little oak.

There are several kinds of wallflowers. The one called red[28] (whose meaning is *chagrin* or *disappointment*) is grown in the southern parts of Europe. It blooms in all seasons. We cultivate it in our gardens to obtain varieties with double flowers of various colours. The yellow wallflower grows on old walls and in the ruins of buildings. Its meaning is preference. The white wallflower symbolises simplicity.

LA GLACIALE*

Iceplant *(Mesembryanthemum crystallinum)*

Indifference

A nymph, as insensitive as she was beautiful, had by her coldness reduced a tender and faithful lover to despair. Flora, wishing to punish the cruel one, condemned her to appear at her court adorned only with garlands and a bouquet of iceplant, a symbol of her indifference.

GRENADE

Pomegranate

(Punica granatum)

Ambition*

According to the Greeks, the monster Agdistis who was the son of Jupiter and of the rock Agdo mutilated himself and the pomegranate was born from the blood which flowed from his

---

28. Probably *Matthiola incana* – 10 weeks stock.

wound.[29] The pomegranate plays quite a large role in Pluto's love story, too. Ceres' daughter, Proserpina, was kidnapped by Pluto, and Ceres came to beg the king of the gods to restore her daughter to her. Jupiter consented, provided that the young beauty had eaten no food since her entry into the underworld. Unfortunately she had sucked a few seeds from a pomegranate. Denounced by Ascalaphus[30], she was condemned by Jupiter to stay with her devilish husband. The informer, however, experienced the vengeance of Proserpina, who transformed him into an owl. There are several species of pomegranates. The common pomegranate is an evergreen and its foliage resembles that of the myrtle. Its appearance is beautiful, especially when it is laden with flowers which begin to bloom in July and follow one another for several months.

HÉLIOTROPE

Heliotrope *(Heliotropium)*
Voluptuousness*. Abandonment*

There are two kinds of heliotropes. The true heliotrope is found on waste land, growing along paths and at the foot of buildings. Its stem is greenish white. The other species of heliotrope is that of Peru[31], brought

---

29. Other versions say it was an almond tree or purple violets that grew from the blood.

30. The custodian of the orchard of Hades.

31. *Heliotropium arborescens.*

to France by Mr. Joseph Jussieu[32]. Its flowers are bluish. The heliotrope, when placed in beautiful vases, perfumes our apartments. It is so laden with dew when the sun is at its strongest that, in half an hour, one can draw two ounces from a single flower. Ovid informs us that Clytie, daughter of Orchame, king of Babylon, was loved by Apollo[33], who then abandoned her for her sister Leucothoea. Clytie felt such pain that she starved herself to death. Apollo, affected by his fatal deed, turned her into a heliotrope.[34]

A SHORT VERSE HAS BEEN OMITTED HERE

HORTENSIA

HYDRANGEA *(Hortensia opuloides)*
CONSTANT LOVE*

A VERSE HAS BEEN OMITTED HERE

---

32. Joseph de Jussieu (1704–1779), a French botanist and explorer.

33. The sun god.

34. This is not quite correct. In his version of this Greek myth, the Roman poet Ovid (43 BCE - c. 18 CE) said that, after Apollo left her for her sister, Clytie told her father, the king of Babylon. His response was to order that Leucothea be buried alive. Grief stricken by what she had done, Clytie remained outside, constantly turning her face towards the sun. Her legs took root and she was transformed into a heliotrope.

Here is a pretty fable on the rose and the hydrangea:

Two men grew flowers,
One was a fool, the other was wise;
One lived in grandeur,
The other lived as a hermit.
The rich man in his garden
Built a large greenhouse;
The pauper with his hand
In the open field, traced out his flowerbed.
The hydrangea, in the former,
Spread its odourless head;
The rose, in the gardener's,
Collected the tears of the dawn.
From Japan the useless flower
Was nothing more than a stranger.
Because of its brilliance and its scent,
Venus held the rose dear.
The sumptuous hydrangea
Ended up boring her master;
The wise man never forgot
The rose he had brought forth.   M. le Chevalier de ST-AMANT[35]

This flower is native to China. It was brought to Europe around 1790

---

35. This poem can be found in several books of the era but none gives any information about the poet.

and was given the French name *rose du Japon*[36]. The hydrangea charms the eye with the brilliance of its beautiful bunches of flowers.

IMMORTELLE

Everlasting *(Gnaphalium* or *Xeranthemum annuum)*
Eternal constancy[37]

Immortelle is the flower of friendship. Its longevity also means it has been seen to symbolise works of genius. This flower, unalterable in its form and in its colours, remains without fading for several years, even when separated from its stem.

A VERSE HAS BEEN OMITTED HERE

IRIS

Iris
Trust*

The mythologists tell us that Iris was the daughter of Thaumas, son of the Earth. Messenger of Juno, she was placed in Heaven by this goddess as the reward for her services. According to the poets, it is the scarf of Iris that we admire

---

36. Rose of Japan.

37. This is just a slight variation of Delachenaye's 'love without end'.

in the rainbow. Her particular job was to shorten the agony of the unfortunates whom a violent passion led to commit suicide. The iris grew in abundance on the mountains of Macedonia. The ancients took care that it was picked by a chaste person, and they observed on this occasion a host of superstitious practices. One finds in Provence a kind of iris called *oeil de paon*[38], because its flowers look like the disc which is on the tail of the bird sacred to Juno. Among the ancients, the iris was the symbol of eloquence. The scent of this flower resembles that of jasmine. The meaning of the white iris is *ardour*.

JACINTHE*

Hyacinth *(Hyacinthus orientalis)*

Pain, sorrow

Apollo, having been exiled from Heaven, guarded the herds of King Admetus on the banks of the Peneus[39]. Unhappy in love, he found a friend in the young Hyacinth, son of Pierus, who became his companion. One day when they were playing with a discus, Zephyrus,[40] jealous of the preference Hyacinth gave to Apollo, blew Apollo's discus onto the head of Hyacinth. Inconsolable, Apollo changed his friend into a flower which, ever since, has been called Hyacinth.

---

38. Peacock's eye.

39. A river in Greece.

40. God of the west wind.

In the hyacinth a beautiful child breathes:
I recognize in it the son of Pierus;
He still seeks the eyes of Phoebus[41],
He still fears Zephyrus' breath.   PARNY[42]

This flower, native to the Orient, grows at the end of winter, and lives only a few days.

Before Flora's return,
She hastens to bloom,
To avoid again
The breath of the Zephyr.   DEMOUSTIER

JASMIN

Jasmine *(Jasminum)*

Passion*. Voluptuousness*

Jasmine, which is originally from India, is used to form thickets and hedges. The persistent green of its leaves, the beauty of its flowers and the sweet scent which they emit all earn it a distinguished place in ornamental gardens. One virtue of this shrub is that it is never attacked

---

41. Another name for Apollo.

42. Évariste Desiré de Forges, vicomte de Parny (1753 –1814), a French poet.

by any insect.[43] It flowers in June and it stays in bloom until the frosts. There are different species and different colours. Yellow represents happiness, and the one from Spain, sensuality.

LAURIER – in Greek DAPHNÉ
Spurge laurel *(Daphne laureola)*

Daphne was sensitive and beautiful,
Apollo sensitive and handsome;
Between them Love with a stroke of his wings,
Made a spark fly
From his dangerous torch.
Daphne, initially forbidden,
Blushes when she sees Apollo.
He approaches, she avoids him;
But does she flee very quickly?
Love makes sure she doesn't.
The god who follows her,
Congratulates himself on her slowness:
She hesitates, she hesitates,
Modesty hastens her escape
Desire slows her down.
He chases after her,
He is ready to seize her;
She will beg for mercy;

---

43. Nowadays, there is a whole host of insects that can attack jasmine so it seems highly unlikely that there were none in Chambet's time.

A nymph is soon weary
When she runs away from pleasure,
She desires, she dares not . . .
Her father sees her fight,
And by her metamorphosis
Prevents her defeat;
Dapbne did not ask him.
It is Apollo she implores,
The sight of her softens his pain;
And to the lover she adores
Her arms still reach
By changing into branches. [44]   MARMONTEL[45]

Among the ancients, the laurel was mainly devoted to Apollo. It adorned his temples, his altars, and the tripod of the Pythia[46]. Because of

---

44. In Greek mythology, Daphne was a dryad, or tree spirit, and daughter of Peneus, the river god. Eros, the god of love, had been offended by Apollo and, in revenge, shot two arrows, one of which hit Apollo and the other Daphne. The result of this was that Apollo became obsessed with Daphne while she lost all interest in love. Exhausted from running away from Apollo, she called to her father for help and he turned her into a laurel tree.

45. Jean-François Marmontel (1723-1799), French poet, dramatist, novelist, and critic.

46. The three legged seat at Delphi on which the Pythian priestess sat to deliver the oracles of the deity.

the belief that it bestowed poetic genius, Clio and Calliope are depicted crowned with laurel.[47] It was also given to poets and winners of the Olympic Games. Seers known as Daphnephages said they were inspired by Apollo and chewed bay leaves before delivering their oracles. The banks of the Penea[48] are covered with a multitude of laurels. It is believed that this is what made the poets imagine the daughter of this river being changed into this shrub.

LAURIER ROSE

Oleander *(Nerium oleander)*
Beauty.[49] Sweetness*

LAURIER BLANC

This also seems to mean OLEANDER
Indecision to love*

LAURIER THYM

Laurestine *(Viburnum tinus)*
Purity of feeling[50]

---

47. Clio, muse of history; Calliope, muse of epic poetry.

48. A river in Thessaly, a region of Greece.

49. Delachenaye has 'Beauty and goodness'.

50. Delachenaye has just 'purity'.

LAURIER AMANDÉ*

CHERRY LAUREL OR ENGLISH LAUREL *(Prunus laurocerasus)*
VICTORY. TRIUMPH[51]

LIERRE

IVY *(Hedera helix)*
RECIPROCATED TENDERNESS

The crowns consecrated to the god of poetry before Daphne's metamorphosis[52] were formed from ivy or myrtle. Everyone knows this ingenious and touching motto associated with the leaves of the ivy: *I die where I cling.* And this one, created by a friend of a disgraced minister who followed him into exile, with an image of ivy embracing a felled tree: *his fall cannot detach me from him.*

LILAS

LILAC *(Syringa)*
FIRST FEELING OF LOVE

This flower originated in the East Indies but has become acclimatised

---

51. Delachenaye gives this meaning to *laurier franc* – the bay tree.

52. Into a laurel.

in Europe. It ornaments our groves where its appearance is as pleasant as its scent. Wild lilacs are found in hedgerows and in woods.

LE LIS

Lily *(Lilium candidum)*

Grandeur. Purity

It is believed that this flower was brought from the East by Francus[53] son of the Trojan hero Hector. The lily is the emblem of France and the kings of the first dynasty carried a shield strewn with a multitude of *fleur de lis*, (or spearheads.) It was under Charles V[54] that the number was reduced to three. The ancients regarded the lily as the symbol of purity, and believed it was born from the milk of Juno to whom it was consecrated. The mother of the Saviour is most often represented with a branch of lily in one of her hands. There are different varieties of this flower in France and in the New World. The yellow lily[55] has the meaning of *anxiety*, and the pink lily of *vanity*.

Noble son of the sun, the majestic lily
Towards his paternal star, whose fires he braves,

---

53. More commonly called Astyanax.

54. 1500-1558.

55. *Hemerocallis lilioasphodelus.*

He lifts with pride his regal head
He is king of the flowers, and the rose is queen. DE BOISJOLIN[56]

MARJOLAINE

Marjoram *(Origanum majorana)*

Always happy*

According to Pliny, an officer of the household of Cynire, King of Cyprus, had been charged with the care of perfumes but had the misfortune to break some vases committed to his care. He was so saddened by this that he dried up with grief, whereupon the gods changed him into marjoram. However, another story assures us that it was Venus who gave birth to this herb on the banks of the Simoïs[57], and that it owes its happy gifts to this goddess. It is said that, if we lose our sense of smell, marjoram will restore it.

MENTHE

Mint *(Mentha)*

Exalted love*

A nymph of this name was adored by Pluto, and was metamorphosed into this plant by the jealous Proserpina[58].

---

56. Jacques-François-Marie Vieilh de Boisjolin (1760-1841), French politician and poet.

57. A river of the Trojan plain, now called the Dümruk Su.

58. The wife of Pluto.

MUGUET*

LILY OF THE VALLEY *(Convallaria majalis)*
LIGHTNESS. INDIFFERENCE

In the golden age, Muguet was a shepherd,
Of the most gallant and most amiable kind;
Young girls never saw him without risk;
He found few that were unresponsive.
Strength, grace, beauty,
Art of verse, eloquence,
Frivolous yet fêted talent
Dressed with elegance,
Muguet had everything;
Everything that can charm, he had,
And if he had been less fickle,
He would have been perfect.
Alas! he abused his means of pleasing,
And deceived the beauty that yielded to his assault.
Soon he left her,
Even laughed at her tears.
In a happy and charming century,
Where a false oath was never taken,
Such a crime must have seemed appalling:
Love then was not indulgent,
It is now more accommodating.
At the court of the gods, Muguet was therefore indicted:
Venus, still a novice, and full of innocence,
Pleaded for loyalty.
It is beautiful to see beauty

Declare for constancy.

In front of Muguet, with a timid and slow step,

Appeared the maidens

Whom he had tormented.

"Agree," he said laughing,

"That all of them are quite nice:

"What are you complaining about?

"Please can I defend myself?

"Is it my fault? Is it such a great misfortune?

"If these beauties have tender hearts?"

Such a speech surprised, and although audacious,

He made both the judge and the audience laugh.

However, with a serious air,

The opinions were gathered, the sentence was passed,

And suddenly the seductive shepherd,

With a breath of love, saw himself changing into a flower

Who bears the name of the fickle young man.

Then who would believe it! The weeping shepherdesses,

Even those he deceived, forgetting their misfortunes,

All exclaimed: What a pity![59]

Lily of the valley is found in woods, valleys and shrubberies; it also adorns and perfumes our gardens. Its flowers are white, drooping and arranged in the form of clusters.

---

59. Chambet gives no attribution for this verse, but it is part of a poem entitled *La Metamorphose de Muguet* by a seemingly little-known 19th century French author, Philibert-Jerome Passac.

MYRTE*

Myrtle *(Myrtus communis)*
Love. Tender return

When the myrtle is in bloom, it signifies betrayed love.

According to some authors, the name myrtle is derived from the Greek word *myron*, which means perfume.[60] This shrub was consecrated to Venus, after bushy myrtles hid this goddess from the ill humour of a troop of satyrs[61]. The myrtle thrives in hot climates, which serves to explain in an ingenious way the offering we make of it to love. We saw near Trézène, a myrtle under which, from afar, Phaedra watched Hyppolytus on his chariot.[62] In her daydream, the wife of Theseus had pierced the leaves of this

---

60. In fact, the Greek for perfume is *aroma*. And the Greek for scent or smell is *myrodia*. *Myro* means myrrh. The French and English names are derived from the Greek name for the plant – *myrtos*.

61. Debauched woodland gods.

62. Phaedra, Cretan princess and wife of Theseus king of Athens, fell in love with her stepson Hippolytus. When he rejected her, she accused him of rape. Theseus called on Poseidon, the god of the sea, to kill Hippolytus. Then Phaedra committed suicide.

myrtle with her hairpin.[63] Since then, a temple has been built in this place, dedicated to Venus the speculator. Winners at the Olympic Games received a crown of myrtle. Statues of heroes were adorned with it. Virgil assures us that there existed a grove of myrtle in the underworld in which the shades of lovers wandered mournfully. It was there that Aeneas found the unfortunate Queen of Carthage.[64]

NARCISSE

Narcissus *(Narcissus pseudonarcissus)*

Love of oneself

Narcissus, son of Cephisa and Liriope, was famous for his beauty. A crowd of nymphs burned with the tenderest love for him; but his indifference was equal to their tenderness. Unhappy Echo, unable to please him, saw her charms wither with grief. But soon she was avenged. One day, on returning from the hunt, the handsome Narcissus, looking at himself in a fountain, became so in love with himself that he dried up with pain and was changed into the flower that bears his name.

---

63. According to a book about Greece written in the second century by the geographer, Pausanias, there was a myrtle bush in Troezen that still had holes in every leaf – the result of Phaedra stabbing them in an attempt to control her passion.

64. Dido, Queen of Carthage, committed suicide after her lover, the Trojan hero Aenaeas, was ordered to return to Rome by Jupiter, king of the gods.

Avoiding the heat of the fires of day,
Here blooms the unfortunate Narcissus:
He still retains the pallor
Which sorrow spreads on his features;
He loves the shade, appropriate to his worries,
But he fears the water which caused his misfortune. PARNY.

Narcissus likes to grow on the banks of streams, and to reflect its image in the waves, which may partly explain the fable of the ancients. This flower was dedicated to the Furies[65].

A VERSE HAS BEEN OMITTED HERE

The narcissus, flowering in April, is one of the plants with which Flora decorates our gardens at the return of spring.

M. Dubos, in his idylls, while speaking to Narcissus, gives a little advice to our ladies, which, for the honour of their sex, they will hasten to take advantage of.

Victim of mad ardour,
At least you can, through your misfortune,
Instruct and correct our beauties:
Inspire healthy dread
Of those, who like you,
Don't know how to love anything except themselves.

---

65. The Greek goddesses of vengeance.

The same verse, while still addressing Narcissus, also gives advice to men:

Alas! in your blind error,
You don't know the happiness
That one experiences when one loves;
The man in love with himself
Does not know how to make anyone happy
And is not happy himself.
The Fates cut short your days to no avail;
In another form, you still
Keep your fatal delusion;
Faithful lover of streams,
You bloom on the edge of the waters,
Still looking at yourself, and admiring yourself.

Claude l'Etoile[66], an old poet also makes Narcissus speak:

Infatuated with the love of myself,
From the shepherd that I was, I became a flower.
Ah! take advantage of my misfortune,
You whom heaven has adorned with supreme beauty;
And to avoid blows,
Since everyone must love,
Love someone other than yourself.

---

66. Claude l'Etoile was a member of the French Academy in the late 18th century.

OEILLET

Pink or Carnation
(Dianthus)
Sentiment*

Some mythologists give the following story as the origin of this flower. Diana, in a fit of bad humour, tore out the eyes of a shepherd whom she met while hunting. Then she did not know what to do with them but, since on reflection they seemed very pretty to her, she scattered them in the fields. From these seeds came flowers which took the name of *oeillet*[67] – a term of tenderness.

> Kind carnation, it is your breath
> Which charms and penetrates our senses;
> It is you who pour into the plain
> These sweet and lovely scents.
> The perfumed spirits that are exhaled by
> The fresh morning rose,
> For us are less delicious;
> And your sweet and pure smell,
> Is an incense that nature
> Raises in tribute to the heavens.   CONSTANT DUBOS,

Le Grand Condé had fun cultivating carnations in his retreat at

---
67. Little eye,

Chantilly.[68] We know the quatrain that Mlle de Scudery[69] wrote on the subject.

> Seeing these carnations that an illustrious warrior
> Watered, with a hand that won battles,
> Remember that Apollo built walls,
> And don't be surprised that Mars is a gardener.

The heart of big carnations has often concealed furtive notes. Queen Marie Antoinette, a prisoner in the Temple, received one in this way. This adventure inspired M. Constant Dubos to write the following verse:

> When an ill-fated queen
> Lay in an abandoned dungeon,
> Exhausted by the harshness of Fate:
> Discreet and faithful messenger,
> A carnation still allowed
> A ray of happiness to shine for her.

The carnation has many varieties in its colours: white represents *fidelity*; deep scarlet, *horror*; yellow, *disdain*; pink, *a feeling*; crimson,

---

68. Louis II de Bourbon, Prince of Condé, (1621-1686) known as le Grand Condé for his military exploits, was one of Louis XIV's most notable generals. The museum at the Chateau of Chantilly is known as the Musée Condé.

69. Madeleine de Scudéry (1607–1701) was a French novelist,

reciprocity; mixed/variegated, *a refusal to love*, etc. , etc.

ORANGER

Orange tree *(Citrus × sinensis)*

Orange blossom* - Gentleness

The fruit of this tree was famous in antiquity. It was with oranges thrown into the competition that Hippomenes defeated Atalanta in a race.[70] This famous garden guarded by monsters, where the Hesperides saw the son of Alcmene enter as victor,[71] contained a treasury of superb orange trees, from which came the fable of the golden apples.

Originally from China, the orange tree was brought to Europe in the sixteenth century by a Portuguese warrior.[72]

THREE VERSES HAVE BEEN OMITTED HERE

---

70. In Greek mythology Atalanta, who didn't want to get married, challenged her suitors to a race. Being a very fast runner she outran all of them except Hippomenes who distracted her by dropping three 'golden apples' given to him by Aphrodite from the garden of the Hesperides, the nymphs of sunset and evening.

71. The son of Alcmene was Heracles.

72. Bitter oranges had arrived in Europe several centuries earlier, probably brought by Moorish soldiers but sweet oranges were introduced in the early 16th century by merchants.

OREILLE D'OURS

Auricula *(Primula auricula)*

Seduction[73]

The leaves of this plant are very erect. Its flowers are arranged like a parasol, and each forms a particularly flared funnel. Their scent is very sweet. There are auriculas which imitate the sheen of satin or velvet.

PAVOT

poppy *(Papaver)*

Inactivity*

The poppy was dedicated to Proserpina. Ceres was shown holding a handful of ears of corn and poppies in memory of the opium she had taken when her daughter was born.[74] It is the emblem of the god of sleep and the symbol of fertility.

We know several species of poppies: The red poppy, also called *coqueliquot*, (symbolising *pride*)[75] grows among the ears of corn and along the roads. The black poppy, (symbol of *lethargy*) has flowers of different colours. The white poppy, (symbol of *suspicion*), is said to originate from the Orient. It blooms in June but its flowers fall immediately. It is from this poppy that opium is derived. The mixed

---

73. Delachenaye has 'Someone is looking to seduce you'.

74. In Greek myth, Proserpina, daughter of Ceres, was abducted by Pluto, king of the underworld.

75. Although earlier Chambet told us that the *coqueliquot* represents *recognition*.

(variegated) poppy expresses *surprise*; the pink poppy, *vivacity*, and the simple poppy, *thoughtlessness*.

PENSÉE

Pansy *(Viola tricolor)*
Expressive memory*

Sweet pansy, ornament of spring,
One day sees both the birth and the end of your empire;
Thoughts of love that a young girl inspires
Are born faster and last longer.

This flower is just a species of scentless violet, with petals of three colours. For this reason, the Latins gave it the name of *Viola tricolor*. The pansy blooms from the beginning of spring until the end of autumn.

A VERSE HAS BEEB OMITTED HERE

PERCE-NEIGE

Snowdrop *(Galanthus)*
Hope

This flower grows in Hungary and southern parts of Europe. Its Greek name is *galenthus* [sic], which means milk flower since the snowdrop is as white as milk.

Benserade[76] makes the snowdrop speak in the following manner, in verses addressed to Julie de Rambouillet[77].

> Under a veil of silver, the buried earth
> Produces me; despite its coldness,
> The snow preserves my life,
> And gives me its name and its whiteness.

PERVENCHE

Periwinkle *(Vinca)*
Eternal friendship[78]

The periwinkle was the favourite plant of the author of *La Nouvelle Héloïse*[79]. Each time one of these flowers presented itself to the gaze of J. J. Rousseau, the heart of this sensitive man throbbed with pleasure. The periwinkle brought up an image to him and brought back memories to him. Periwinkles make pretty carpets in our winter

---

76. Isaac de Benserade (1612-1691), a French poet.

77. Julie d'Angennes, Duchess of Montausier, and daughter of the Marquise de Rambouillet, was chief lady in waiting to the French queen, Marie Thérèse, from 1664 to 1671.

78. Delachenaye has 'friendship for life'.

79. Jean-Jacques Rousseau (1712-1778) writer and philosopher.

groves. From the month of April, when all the trees are still bare, their flowers, some of which are white, others blue, present to the eye their very beautiful colours.

PIED D'ALOUETTE

Larkspur *(Delphinium consolida or Delphinium ajacis)*
Lightness

Some authors believe that the larkspur is what the ancients referred to as a hyacinth. This plant is native to Asia. Its leaves are green, its top is adorned with spikes of flowers which are sometimes a beautiful azure blue, and sometimes purple, pink or white, etc. The popular legend is that the larkspur was born from the blood of Ajax, after this hero, furious with Odysseus and the Greeks, had pierced himself with his sword.[80]

REINE-MARGUERITE*

China aster *(Callistephus chinensis)*
or Wild daisy *(Leucanthemum heterophyllum)*
Splendour*

The Greek name for this flower is *leucos*, white, and *antheneon*, flower.[81] The *Reine Marguerite* was sent to us from China in

---

80. Ajax was a hero of the Trojan war. He was enraged when the armour of the slain hero, Achilles, was given to Odysseus and not to him. Eventually he committed suicide.

81. Actually the Greek for flower is *anthos*.

1730. This beautiful plant deserves the name of *Reine*[82] because of the brilliance of its flowers and the variety of its colours.

A VERSE HAS BEEN OMITTED HERE

The author of *Etudes de la Nature*[83], in connection with this flower, tells us about an early childhood game. A child pulls off the white petals one after the other, saying: "he loves me a little, passionately, not at all," and so on until the last one. M. Dubos alludes to this banter in the following verses:

Often the shepherdess,
Far from her young lover,
Says to herself: is he faithful to me?
Will he come back constant?
Trembling she picks you......
Under her uncertain finger,
The oracle that she strips of petals
Reveals her destiny.

We find a profusion in our meadows of the flower named *marguerite simple*[84] whose meaning is *regret* or *sadness*.

---

82. Queen.

83. *Nature Studies.*

84. Common daisy.

RENONCULE

Buttercup *(Ranunculus)*
Impatience

This flower was known in the twelfth and thirteenth centuries. The Crusaders had seen them in the East and it was King Louis IX who was the first to bring the buttercup to France on his return from Palestine. The *Renoncule des Fleuristes*[85] holds the same rank among enthusiasts as the carnation, the tulip, the hyacinth, etc. It can be single, double or semi double and these three species include all the varieties. There is a species of *Ranunculus* called anemone which is found in the woods. The creeping buttercup[86] is called *bouton d'or*[87] and has the meaning of wealth.

> Ranunculus one day in a bouquet
> With the carnation was found united:
> The next day she had the perfume of the carnation.....
> You can only profit from good company.   M. BÉRENGER [88]

---

85. Persian buttercup - *Ranunculus asiaticus.*

86. *Ranunculus repens.*

87. Golden button.

88. Possibly Pierre Jean de Beranger (1780-1857), poet and songwriter.

RÉSÉDA

M<small>IGNONETTE</small> *(Reseda odorata/alba/lutea)*
M<small>OMENTARY HAPPINESS</small>

The mignonette perfumes the gardens from spring to autumn. Its winding stem, which is almost creeping, is of a pale green. Its leaves have no regularity to their form, and are soft and gentle to the touch. The flowers of the mignonette form a rounded spike and look like so many miniatures. They always lie in a sloping direction.

ROMARIN

R<small>OSEMARY</small> *(Rosmarinus officinalis)*
H<small>ONESTY, CANDOUR</small>

This flower, disregarded today, was well known to the ancients. It was part of the perfumes they used. Its penetrating aroma adds to feelings of love and pleasure. It was once included in the composition of bouquets and of hats of flowers, and was intertwined in wreaths of myrtle and laurel. It is one of the plants used most successfully in aromatic baths. It contains in the bottom of its calyx [the green part that surrounds the petals when in bud] a honeyed substance which attracts bees from afar. Rosemary grows wild in all hot countries. Its flowers are small, pale blue and sweet smelling.

ROSE

ROSE*

FRESHNESS. TENDERNESS

This flower, queen of our gardens was – according to Anacreon[89] – born when Venus left the bosom of the empire of Amphitrite[90]. The names Rhodante[91] and Rhodes[92] are derived from a Greek word which means rose[93].

A VERSE HAS BEEN OMITTED HERE

The crimson of the rose is attributed to the blood of Venus. This distraught goddess flew to the aid of her dear Adonis when he lay mortally wounded. Thorny rose bushes were in her path and tore her breast, so that several drops of her blood spurted on the roses. These flowers, which had hitherto been white, have since preserved the colour of the blood of Venus.

A VERSE HAS BEEN OMITTED HERE

---

89. A Greek poet who lived c. 575 – c. 495.

90. Amphitrite was the Greek goddess of the sea.

91. A Greek woman who in the 5th century BCE sponsored the dramatist Thespis.

92. The largest of the Greek Dodecanese islands.

93. The Greek word for rose is *rodo*.

The poet Contant Dubos said of the rose:

To beauty belongs the adornment:
Only she has the right to pick you;
And only you can beautify
Nature's masterpiece.
Your crimson form arises,
The throne on which love rests;
Rose, on the breast of a rose,
Will shine with new brilliance.
The Graces crown the heads
Of your buds newly formed,
When from Gnidus[94] and Paphos[95]
Their presence embellishes the celebrations.
Venus entwines you with her hair,
Love accepts you as an offering;
You form the garland of Hebe[96]
When she offers the cup to the gods.

---

94. A city in Caria, modern day Turkey, renowned for a statue of Venus by the Greek sculptor Praxiteles in the 4th century BCE.

95. A city in Cyprus.

96. The goddess of youth and cupbearer to the gods on Mount Olympus.

In vain, cold reason

Rejects metempsychosis; [97]

I believe I breathe in the rose the soul of the tender Anacreon[98].

TWO VERSES HAVE BEEN OMITTED HERE

Gentil Bernard[99] begins an Anacreontic ode[100] to the rose with these lines:

Tender fruit of Aurora's tears,

Object of Zephyr's kisses,

Queen of the empire of Flora,

Make speed to flourish.

What am I saying, alas! Postpone,

Postpone a moment before opening.

The moment in which you bloom

Is the one that causes you to wither.

Nothing is more melancholy and, at the same time, more gracious than these verses of Malherbe, to his friend Duperrier, on the death of a

---

97. The transmigration at death of the soul into another body.

98. A Greek poet who lived c. 575 – c. 495.

99. Pierre-Joseph Bernard (1708–1775) was a French soldier and poet who wrote discreet erotic verse which resulted in him being nicknamed Gentil-Bernard by Voltaire.

100. ie written in the style of Anacreon.

beloved daughter:

> Alas! she was from the world where the most beautiful things
> Have the worst fate:
> And like a rose she lived as roses live,
> The space of a morning.

A SHORT VERSE HAS BEEN OMITTED HERE

This lovely flower inspired M. Armand Gouffé[101] to write the following couplet, a sort of madrigal which is addressed as much to the beauties as to the queen of our flowerbeds.

> As soon as the heat comes
> Zephyr, with his light wings,
> Opens the chalices of flowers
> And the girdles of our shepherdesses.
> In all places and at all times
> Love arranges things well;
> He knows that everywhere, in the spring,
> We must see rosebuds,

THREE VERSES HAVE BEEN OMITTED HERE

> Soon in the groves of the superb Orient,
> That most beautiful of flowers, the rose, will appear;
> It opens and immediately its perfume spreads.

---

101. Armand Gouffé (1775–1845) was a French poet.

The garden nymph, surprised at seeing it,
Believes that, on this day, another Venus has just been born.
We seek to recognize her as the queen of flowers;
The rose is astonished; a likeable modesty
Covers her charming breast with a vivid blush.
The nightingale sees her, beats the air with his wings,
Breathes in her perfumes, flutters on her breast,
Sings of happy love, and suddenly flies away,
Although he swore always to be faithful. AIMÉ MARTIN[102]

A VERSE HAS BEEN OMITTED HERE

A woman is like a rose
Which is born in the morning of a beautiful day
And which only completely blooms
With the breath of love.

ROSE BLANCHE
White rose
Interest. Innocence

You whose glory is to be beautiful,
Young flower of a lovable sex,
Take the rose as a model,
Its brilliance comes from its modesty.

---

102. Aimé Martin (1781-1844) was a French writer.

This ornament of nature
Hides under a shrub,
And to keep her beauty pure,
Arms her cradle with thorns.   M. de LEGRE[103]

We remember the ancient custom of Saint Médard, which consisted of crowning a virgin every year in the church of Salency.[104] The prize for her virtue was a simple hat of white roses.[105]

We think it our duty to recall those white roses and red roses which played such a great part during the civil disturbances which afflicted England in the fifteenth century. We know that the red rose eventually succumbed.[106] When the white rose is withered, its meaning is: *Rather die than lose innocence.*

---

103. The identity of the poet is unknown. One source attributes this poem to 'Lamparelli' – also unknown – and another says 'translated from the Italian'.

104. St Médard (c. 456–545) was born in Salency, a village some 70 miles north of Paris, and became the Bishop of Noyon. It is said that he crowned his sister Médrine as the first 'Rosière'.

105. The ceremony is still enacted each year, with the *Rosière* being escorted to Mass by 12 girls and 12 boys. She is crowned with 12 roses and receives a bouquet of roses and other gifts. The whole village joins in the celebrations.

106. In the Wars of the Roses, the Yorkists had a white rose as their emblem, while the Lancastrians had a red rose.

A POEM HAS BEEN OMITTED HERE

ROSE JAUNE

Yellow rose

Shame, disgrace.

Infidelity

The yellow flowered rose is said to be native to the Orient. It grows in England, Germany and the southern part of France. Its flowers, which are always double, are of a more or less light yellow, or of a dark poppy red.[107]

ROSE SAUVAGE

Wild rose

Simplicity*

The wild rose, also called *églantier*, is a shrub that grows in hedges and woods. It produces single roses of very short duration, of a white and crimson colour. If the rose with its thorns has the meaning of *marriage*, the one which is without thorns, represents *a sincere friend*.

---

107. It seems that Chambet is referring here to a specific species of rose which, although he calls it a 'yellow flowered rose' – 'rosier à fleurs jaunes' – is not necessarily yellow.

The musk rose has *caprice* as its emblem.

The variegated rose), *betrayed love*.

The rosebud, *a heart that ignores love*.

The Austrian copper rose *(Rosa foetida) love of the fine arts*

SCABIEUSE

Scabious

Cruel abandonment*

The scabious which grows in our gardens is brown – golden brown on the edges and black in the central florets. This flower is also a lover of woods. One of its varieties was sacred to the Oreads.[108] It is also found in fields, but it is rare. Scabious is also called *veuve*.[109] It is solitary and bent at the end of a long stem.

SENSITIVE

Sensitive plant *(Mimosa pudica)*

Sensitivity[110]

The sensitive plant has been given the Latin name of *Mimosa pudica*[111] because it seems to imitate the simpering of an actress. The sensitive plant is also native to the southern parts of the New World.

---

108. Greek mountain nymphs.

109. Widow.

110. Delachenaye gives a meaning of *secret and profound sensitivity*.

111. *Pudica* meaning chaste.

The ancients told this story of its origin: Pan fell in love with a young nymph from Diana's retinue. This chaste and timid beauty opposed his love with an unassailable resistance. Finally, one day when the cloven footed god was about to triumph with the help of violence, Diana came to the aid of her nymph, and transformed her into the sensitive plant.

> And this solitary plant
> Modestly teaches you the rules,
> Fending off the reckless touch,
> On itself you see it
> Fold back to escape,
> And, by a salutary instinct,
> Keep its foliage away from your breath, from your fingers.

A VERSE HAS BEEN OMITTED HERE

SÉRINGA*

MOCK ORANGE *(Philadelphus coronarius)*
CONTEMPT

The elegant shrub called mock orange exhales the scent of orange. Its Latin name *Philadelphus*[112] seems to relate to the intertwining of its branches, or to the bringing together of its flowers. This shrub grows easily into a bush. Its stems are loaded with numerous small green

---

112. From the Greek *philos,* meaning friend, and *adelphos,* meaning brother.

branches. The dark green leaves of the mock orange do not play in the breeze – they have a kind of stiffness in their texture. The white flowers of mock orange crowd at the end of each branch, alternating with each other on their short peduncles, with a terminal flower completing the charming group.

SOUCI*

Marigold *(Calendula officinalis)*

Pain. Torment

We find in a modern work this somewhat complicated motto, which was created to express jealousy: A marigold flower, exposed to a burning mirror which receives the rays of the sun, and which reflects them onto her: *I die, because he is watching you*.

Proserpine was, it is said, picking marigolds at the foot of Mount Etna, when the monarch of the underworld, enamoured of her charms, carried her away and led her to his dark abode.

A VERSE HAS BEEN OMITTED HERE

Indeed, the marigold gives off an unpleasant odour, which is spread to our fingers if we touch it. Marigold flowers close at sunset and open at sunrise on calm days. A curious observation has been made about the marigold: in the height of summer, half an hour after sunset if the atmosphere is clean, the marigold flower shoots out sparks and flashes. This phenomenon is probably due to electricity.

TOURNESOL

S UNFLOWER *(Helianthus annuus)*
I NTRIGUE*

The sunflower or great sun, called in Latin *Helianthus*[113] is native to Virginia. It has been growing in our beds for a long time. Its flowers, made up of yellow rays around a brown disc, bear a resemblance to the way the sun is depicted. It is said that a sunflower can produce up to four thousand seeds.

TROÈNE

P RIVET *(Ligustrum vulgare)*
D EFENCE, PROHIBITION

The privet grows in woods. The leaves of this shrub are of a beautiful green. Its flowers, which are of an admirable whiteness, spread a sweet smell. Their brilliance is transient like that of the rose. Privet berries are eaten by small birds.

---

113. From the Greek *helios* meaning sun and *anthos* meaning flower.

TUBÉREUSE

TUBEROSE
(Polianthes tuberosa)
INDIFFERENCE*

This flower is none other than the hyacinth of the Indies, brought to Europe by a certain Francus who traded on various seas. The tuberose is the most fragrant autumn flower. Roucher[114] speaks of a woman who became an imbecile after inhaling the perfumes of this flower too keenly.

TULIPE

TULIP *(Tulipa gesneriana)*
HONESTY

There are two kinds of tulips – the first which are called wild tulips, and those known as florists' tulips. They differ in shape. Those of the woods are not variegated. They bloom in the spring and are found in marshes, grasslands and forests. The double tulip has the meaning of friendship. Mythologists have claimed that this flower was once a nymph, companion of Flora, and the object of Zephyr's love.

A POEM ABOUT THIS MYTH HAS BEEN OMITTED HERE

---

114. Jean-Antoine Roucher (1745-1794) was a French poet who was guillotined towards the end of the French Revolution.

LA VIOLETTE

Violet

Reserve.* Modesty

Io, a nymph in Diana's retinue, was loved by the sun god Apollo. When she constantly resisted his love, he became indignant and turned her into a violet, a flower which still shuns brightness and which has become the symbol of a pure virgin, seeking to hide from the sight of the profane. Others claim that the land affected by Io's misfortunes gave birth to this flower under her feet to console her in her woe. Vulcan, the Roman god of fire, being unable to please Venus[115] covered his forehead with violets, and adorned the bed and the apartment of Cytherea[116] with these flowers. Sensitive then to this sweet perfume, the goddess smiled gracefully, opened her beautiful arms, and bringing her celestial mouth to that of Vulcan, intoxicated him with ravishing kisses.

A VERSE HAS BEEN OMITTED HERE

Without pomp and without admirers,
You live obscure, abandoned,
And the eye is still looking for your flower
When the sense of smell has detected it.
Under the ungrateful feet of passers-by
Often you perish defenceless;
So under the blows of the wicked
Sometimes humble innocence dies.   CONST. DUBOS

---

115. His wife.

116. Another name for Venus.

This flower played a famous role in the revolutionary troubles of 1815.[117] The white violet* has *innocence* as its meaning; yellow, *perfect beauty*; the double violet, *reciprocal friendship*; a violet surrounded by leaves, *hidden love*.

It has been said of the violet compared to the rose:
Don't wait for the brilliant successes
That the purple rose obtains;
You are not the flower of lovers,
But, equally, you have no thorn.

A woman who was as witty as she was amiable, but of a shy and reserved character, took this flower as her emblem with these words: *you must look for me*.

The poet Régnier-Démarais[118] addressed the following verses to Madame de Rambouillet[119] in which the personified violet is expressed thus:

Modest in my colour, modest in my stay,
Free of ambition I hide under the grass,

---

117. After Napoleon was exiled to Elba his supporters started to wear violets as a secret symbol of their allegiance.

118. François-Séraphin Régnier-Desmarais (1632-1713), a French priest, diplomat and poet.

119. Catherine de Vivonne, marquise de Rambouillet (1588-1665). She hosted literary salons attended by the great writers of the time.

But if on your forehead I can see myself one day,
The most humble of flowers will be the most superb.
.

You announce to me, oh violet,
The brilliant court of spring:
You appear, I hear the warbler
And soft breezes embellish our fields.
The primrose emerges out of the grass,
Unfolding its flower clusters.
What good is her superb luxury to her?
She doesn't have your sweet smell.

INDEX OF PLANT NAMES

Acacia (Acacia) 88
Acanthus (Acanthe) 88, 123
Aconite (Aconite) 51, 124
Almond tree (Amandier) 89, 124
Aloes (Aloës) 88
Amaranth (Amarante) 89, (Amaranthe) 125, (Immortelle) 101
Amaryllis (Amaryllis) 26, 89, 125
Anemone (Anémone) 63, 89, 126
Anemone, wild (Anémone sauvage) 89
Anemone, wood (Sylvie) 59
Angel trumpets (Belle-de-nuit) 91, 129
Angelica (Angélique) 127
Ash tree (Frêne) 99
Auricula (Oreille-d'ours) 53, 107, 161
Balm (Baume) 91
Balsam (Balsamine) 90,128, (Balsamine des jardins) 49,
Barberry (Epine vinette) 61, 97

Basil (Basilic) 91, 129

Bay leaf - see Laurel leaf

Bear's breeches – see Acanthus

Bear's ear – see Auricula

Beech mast or nuts (Faine) 97

Bell flower (Uvularia) 44, (Campanelle) 93, (Clochette) 95, 135

Bilberry (Airelle anguleuse) 48

Bindweed – see Morning glory

Bittersweet (Douce-amère) 96

Bladder senna (Baguenaudier) 90

Bluebell (Coucou) 136

Bluebottle – see Cornflower

Borage (Bourrache) 92

Box (Buis) 92

Bramble (Ronce) 110

Brazilian cress – see Toothache plant

Broom (Genét) 137, (Genêt d'espagne) 99

Bulrush – see Rush

Burning bush – see Dittany, white

Buttercup (Bouton d'or) 27, 92, 133 (Renoncule) 110, 166

Buttercup, Persian (Renoncule des fleuristes) 41

Camomile (Camomille) 93

Cardamon (Amomum) 89

Carnation (Oeillet) 56, 158

Carnation, pink (Oeillet rose) 106

Carnation, variegated (Oeillet panache) 106

Carnation, white (Oeillet blanc) 106

Castor oil plant (Ricin) 68

Cedar (Cèdre) 93

Celandine (Chélidoine) 75, 94

Cherry blossom (Fleur de cerisier) 98

Chestnut blossom (Fleur de morronnier) 98

Chimney bellflower (Pyramidale) 109

China aster (Reine-marguerite) 42, 164 (Marguerite Reine) 104,

China pink (Oeillet de Chine) 30, 106

Christ's thorn (Paliure) 67

Chrysanthemum (Chrysanthème) 94

Cinnamon (Cinnamomum) 94

Cinquedfoil (Quintefeuille) 40

Clematis, fragrant (Vigne blanche) 35

Clover, white (Coucou) 136

Cockscomb (Amarante-passe-velours or Crete-de-coq) 69

Columbine (Ancolie) 60, 89

Convolvulus (Convolvulus) 95

Corn lily (Ixia) 37

Corn, ears of (Epis) 97

Cornflower (Bluet or Barbeau) 75, 133 (Barbeau-bleu) 90,

Cornflower, cultivated (Barbeau-bleu des jardins) 90

Cowslip (Primevère) 109

Crowfoot - see Buttercup

Crown imperial (Fritillaire imperiale) 32, (Impériale) 101,
   (Couronne imperiale) 136

Cyclamen (Cyclamen d'europe) 55

Cypress tree (Cyprès) 96

Daffodil - see Narcissus

Daisy (Marguerite) 38, 104

Daisy, ox eye (Marguerite blanche) 104

Daisy, tricolour (Chrysanthème caréné) 53

Daisy, wild (Reine-marguerite) 164
Dandelion (Dent-de-lion) 96
Darnel (Ivraie) 101
Day lily (Belle-de-jour) 91
Dead nettle, white (Ortie blanche) 107
Delphinium – see Larkspur
Dittany, white (Dictame blanc) 49
Ebony tree (Ebénier) 96
Elder (Sureau) 113
Elm tree (Orme) 107
Everlasting (Xéranthème) 46, (Immortelle) 101, 143
Fair maid of France (Bouton-d'argent) 92
Fir tree (Sapin) 112
Fireweed – see Willowherb, great
Flag, common – see Iris, German
Flax flower (Fleur de lin) 98
Forget me not (Myosotis) 105
Foxglove (Digitale) 96
Foxglove, purple (Digitale pourpre) 29
Fraxinella – see Dittany, white
Fumitory (Fumeterre) 99
Geranium (Géranium) 99, 138
Geranium, zonal (Géranium à zones) 34
Germander (Germandrée) 99, 138
Gillyflower (Giroflée) 138
Gillyflower, red (Giroflée rouge) 100
Goldenrod (Verge d'or) 45
Goosegrass – see Silverweed
Grass (Gramen) 100

THE LANGUAGE OF FLOWERS 1810-1816   187

Guelder rose (Boule-de-neige) 66, 92, 132
Hawthorn (Aubépine) 50, 90, 128
Heather (Bruyère) 92
Heliotrope (Héliotrope) 100, 140
Heliotrope of Peru (Héliotrope du Pérou) 34
Hellebore (Ellébore) 97
Hellebore, stinking (Pied-de-griffon) 73
Hemlock (Ciguë) 94
Hemp agrimony (Eupatoire) 57
Herb Robert (Bec-de-grue) 91
Hibiscus (Ketmie) 37
Hollyhock (Althéa) 88, (Rose Trémière) 112
Honeysuckle (Chèvre-feuille) 58, 94, 134
Hops (Houblon) 101
House leek (Joubarbe) 103
Hyacinth (Hyacinthe or Jacinthe) 72 , (Hyacinthe) 101,
              (Jacinthe) 144
Hydrangea (Hortensia) 69, 101, 141
Iceplant (Glaciale) 139
Iris (Iris) 101, 143
Iris, German (Iris flambe or Iris de Germanie) 36
Ivy (Lierre) 103, 149
Jacob's ladder (Echelle-de-jacob) 52
Jasmine (Jasmin) 145
Jasmine, lemon-scented (Jasmin des Açores) 102
Jasmine, Spanish (Jasmin d'espagne) 36, 102
Jasmine, white (Jasmin blanc) 102
Jasmine, yellow (Jasmin jaune) 102
Jerusalem cherry (Pomme d'amour) 63

Jerusalem thorn – see Christ's thorn
Jonquil (Jonquille) 60, 102
Juniper (Genièvre) 99
Kidney vetch (Coucou) 136
Lady's bedstraw (Caille-lait) 93
Larkspur (Pied d'alouette) 65, 109, 164
Laurel (Laurier) 146 (Laurier franc) 103
Laurel leaf (Feuille de laurier) 97
Laurel, cherry (Laurier amandé) 149
Laurel, English – see Laurel, cherry
Laurel, white (Laurier blanc) 103
Laurestine (Laurier thym) 103, 148
Lemon balm (Citronnelle) 95
Lemon tree (Citronnier) 95, 134
Lilac (Lilas) 25, 103, 149
Lily (Lis) 150
Lily of the valley (Muguet) 47, 152
Lily, Madonna (Lis blanc) 38, 104
Lily, pink (Lis rose) 104
Lily, yellow (Lis Jaune) 104
Liverwort (Hépatique) 100
Lotus (Lotus) 104
Lychnis, scarlet (Croix-de-Jérusalem) 95
Maidenhair fern (Cheveux-de-Vénus) 94
Mallow (Althéa) 88, (Mauve) 105
Marigold (Souci) 177, (Souci d'espagne) 64
Marigold, French (Oeillet d'inde) 106
Marjoram (Marjolaine) 105, 151
Marvel of Peru (Belle-de-nuit) 91, 129

THE LANGUAGE OF FLOWERS 1810–1816   189

Meadowsweet (Ulmaire) 66, (Reine-des-près) 110
Michaelmas daisy, European (Oeil-de-christ) 58
Mignonette (Réséda) 110, 167
Mint (Menthe) 105, 151
Mock orange (Séringa) 176
Monkshood – see Aconite
Morning glory (Liseron) 38, (Belle-de-jour) 91, 130
Mullein, great (Bouillon-blanc) 92
Mushroom (Champignon) 93
Myrtle (Myrte) 61, 154
Narcissus (Narcisse) 39, 106, 155
Nasturtium (Capucine) 93, 134
Nightshade (Belle-de-nuit) 91
Oak (Chêne) 94
Oleander (Laurier Rose) 103, 148 (Laurier blanc) 148
Olive (Olive) 107
Olive tree (Olivier) 107
Orange (Orange) 107
Orange blossom (Fleur d'oranger) 98, 160
Orange tree (Oranger) 40, 160
Oxlip (Coucou) 136
Palm tree (Palmier) 108
Pansy (Pensée) 76, 108, 162
Passion flower (Fleur de passion) 98
Peach blossom (Fleur de pêcher) 98
Pearly everlasting, common
       (Immortelle Blanche or Gnaphale De Virginie) 61
Pennycress (Thlaspie) 113
Peony (Pivoine) 41, 109

Periwinkle (Pervenche) 108, 163, (Pervenche, grande) 54

Pheasant's eye, summer (Adonis d'ete) 28

Phlox (Phlox) 32

Pine tree (Pin) 109

Pink – see Carnation

Pink, garden (Mignardise) 105

Plane tree (Platane) 109

Pomegranate flower (Grenade fleur) 100

Pomegranate fruit (Grenade fruit) 100

Pomegranate (Grenade) 139

Pomegranate tree (Grenadier) 33

Poplar tree (Peuplier) 108

Poppy (Coquelicot) 27, (Pavot) 161

Poppy, opium (Pavot) 108

Poppy, wild (Coquelicot) 95, 135

Pride of Ohio – see Shootingstar, common

Primrose (Prime-vère) 54, (Coucou) 136

Privet (Troène) 114, 178

Rhododendron, American – see Rose bay

Rock rose (Ciste) 28

Rose (Rose) 168, (Rose de jardin) 111

Rose bay (Rododendron, grand) 68

Rose campion (Coquelourde) 66

Rose, Austrian copper (Rose Capucine) 111

Rose, cabbage (Rose à cent feuilles) 39

Rose, dog (Eglantier) 30

Rose, French (Rose de Provins) 71

Rose, musk (Rose musquée) 111

Rose, thornless (Rose sans épine) 111

Rose, variegated (Rose panache) 111
Rose, white (Rose blanche) 110, 172
Rose, white dried (Rose blanche desséchée) 110
Rose, wild (Rose sauvage) 112, 174
Rose, yellow (Rose jaune) 111, 174
Rosebud (Rose en bouton) 111
Rosemary (Romarin) 110, 167
Rush (Jonc) 102
Sage (Sauge) 112
Scabious (Scabieuse) 43, 112, 175
Scurvy Grass (Cochléaria) 95
Sensitive Plant (Sensitive) 43, 113, 175
Shootingstar, common (Dodécathéon) 70
Silverweed (Argentine) 50, 90, 128
Snapdragon (Muffle-de-veau) 105
Snowball – see Guelder rose
Snowdrop (Perce-neige) 108, 162
Solomon's seal (Sceau-de-Salomon) 112
Speedwell (Véronique) 114
Spindle tree (Fusain) 99
St John's wort (Millepertuis) 76, 105
Star of Bethlehem, pyramidal (Ornithogale pyramidale) 64
Strawberry (Fraisier) 48
Strawberry flower (Fleur de fraisier) 98
Sunflower (Soleil or Tournesol) 52, (Soleil) 113,
                (Tournesol) 114, 178
Sweet briar (Eglantier) 97
Sweet pea (Pois-de-senteur) 59, 109
Sweet sultan, yellow (Ambrette or Barbeau jaune) 68

Sweet william (Oeillet-de –Poète) 74, 106

Sycamore tree (Sycomore) 113

Ten weeks stock (Quarantain or Giroflée quarantaine 67

Thistle (Chardon) 93

Thistledown (Aigrette) 88

Thorn (Epine) 97

Thorn apple, purple (Datura violet) 96

Thorn apple, white (Datura blanc) 96

Thuja (Thuya) 113

Thyme (Thym) 114

Thyme, wild (Serpolet) 113

Toothache plant (Abécédaire) 25

Touch me not – see Sensitive

Trumpet Creeper (Jasmin de Virginie) 102

Tuberose (Tubéreuse) 59, 114, 179

Tulip (Tulipe) 114, 179, (Tulipe Des Fleuristes) 44

Violet (Violette) 73, 115, 180

Violet surrounded by leaves (Violette entourée de feuilles) 115

Violet, double (Violette double) 114

Violet, yellow (Violette jaune) 115

Virginia spiderwort (Éphémère de Virginie) 31

Wallflower (Quarantain or Giroflée quarantaine) 67, (Giroflée) 138

Wallflower, yellow (Rameau d'or) 51, (Giroflée jaune) 100

Water pepper (Persicaire) 108

Watsonia, wild (Antholyze éclatante) 62

Weeping willow (Saule pleureur) 112

Whortleberry – see Bilberry

Willow (Osier) 107

Willowherb, great (Nériette) 57

Wormwood (Absinthe) 88, (Absynthe) 123
Xeranthemum (Immortelle) 101
Yucca (Yucca) 45
Zinnia, Peruvian (Zinnia rouge) 47

ACKNOWLEDGMENTS

All the illustrations in this book are based on photographs. One or two of the original photographs were taken by the author, but most of them were taken by talented photographers who generously share their work online under a variety of licences. Attribution for each of these photos is given below, with the publishers' thanks. Each shows (in square brackets) the type of licence under which the photo is shared and/or the website on which it appears.

Page 25   ABECEDAIRE   Jeevan Jose, Kerala, India   [CC BY-SA 4.0]
Page 28   ADONIS D'ETE   Gideon Pisanty (Gidip)   [CC BY-SA 3.0]
Page 30   OEILLET DE LA CHINE   Mokkie   [CC BY-SA 4.0]
Page 32   FRITILLAIRE IMPERIALE   Radoslaw Ziomber
          [CC BY-SA 3.0]
Page 35   VIGNE BLANCHE   Dinesh Valke   [CC BY-SA 2.0]
Page 37   KETMIE   Hat-spass-gemacht on https://pixabay.com/
Page 41   PIVOINE   https://www.pxfuel.com/
Page 44   TULIPE DES FLEURISTES   Easterstockphotos   [CC BY 3.0]
Page 46   XERANTHEME   Stefan.lefnaer   [CC BY-SA 4.0]
Page 47   MUGUET   berger_anja on https://pixabay.com/
Page 50   AUBEPINE   https://www.pxfuel.com/

THE LANGUAGE OF FLOWERS 1810–1816   195

Page 55   Cyclamen d'Europe   Dominicus Johannes Bergsma [CC BY-SA 4.0]

Page 60   Ancolie   2017343 on https://pixabay.com/

Page 62   Antholyze eclatante   Andrew Massyn [CC BY-SA 3.0]

Page 65   Pied d'alouette   Bestenz_2017 on https://pixabay.com/

Page 72   Hyacinthe   WebLab24_Siti_Web on https://pixabay.com/

Page 75   Chelidoine   Anne Burgess [CC BY 2.0]

Page 88   Absinthe   ☐☐ HQ [CC BY-SA 2.0]

Page 89   Amandier   Matthiasboeckel on https://pixabay.com/

Page 90   Argentine   Ghislain118 http://www.fleurs-des-montagnes.net [CC BY-SA 3.0]

Page 91   Basilic   Freefoodphotos [CC BY 3.0]

Page 92   Bouillon-blanc   Vinayaraj [CC BY-SA 4.0]

Page 93   Caille-lait   Peter O'Connor [CC BY-SA 2.0] on https://www.flickr.com/

Page 94   Chelidoine   Andrew Curtis [CC BY 2.0] on https://www.geograph.org.uk/

Page 95   Citronelle   Broly0 [CC0 1.0]

Page 96   Cyprès   Kristofz [CC BY 4.0]

Page 97   Eglantier   WikimediaImages on https://pixabay.com/

Page 98   Fleur de cerisier   Hunter Harmon on https://www.pexels.com/

Page 99   Frene   Brian Green on https://www.geograph.org.uk/

Page 100   Giroflee jaune   Gaimard on https://pixabay.com/

Page 101   Hortensia   Σ64 [CC BY 4.0]

Page 102   Jasmin blanc   https://www.pxfuel.com/

Page 103   Joubarbe   Hans on https://pixabay.com/

Page 104 Lis blanc Cimi [CC0] on https://pxhere.com/
Page 105 Marjolaine maky.orel on https://pixabay.com/
Page 106 Narcisse John c. Akers jr. on https://www.flickr.com/
Page 107 Olive Вbласенко [CC BY-SA 3.0]
Page 108 Palmier [CC0] on https://pxhere.com/
Page 109 Pied-d'alouette Ryan Hodnett [CC BY-SA 4.0]
Page 110 Reine-des-pres Peter O'Connor aka anemoneprojectors [CC BY-SA 2.0]
Page 111 Rose capucine A. Barra [CC BY-SA 3.0]
Page 112 Rose sauvage Jonathan Billinger on https://www.geograph
Page 113 Sensitive Johan [CC BY-SA 3.0]
Page 114 Thym Sigmund on https://unsplash.com/
Page 115 Violette entouree de feuilles gailhampshire [CC BY 2.0] on https://www.flickr.com/
Page 123 Absynthe Matt Lavin on https://www.flickr.com/
Page 125 Amaranth Wildfeuer [CC BY-SA 3.0]
Page 130 Belle-de-nuit Peganum [CC BY-SA 2.0]
Page 133 Bouton d'or https://pxhere.com/
Page 137 Genet Des Colhoun on https://www.geograph.org.uk/
Page 139 Grenade Ken Bosma [CC BY 2.0] on https://www.flickr.com/
Page 143 Iris Frank Mayfield [CC BY-SA 2.0]
Page 149 Lierre Mokkie [CC BY-SA 3.0]
Page 154 Myrte Jonathan Billinger [CC BY-SA 2.0]
Page 158 Oeillet https://www.rawpixel.com/
Page 163 Pervenche https://pxhere.com/
Page 166 Renoncule G. Renard [CC BY 2.0]
Page 179 Tubereuse Swaminathan from Gurgaon [CC BY 2.0]

Printed in Great Britain
by Amazon